Double T-Double Cross

The Firing of Coach Mike Leach: The Backroom Deal That Deflated the Red Raider Nation

By

Michael Lee Lanning

SCOTTSDALE
Book Publishing, LLC

ISBN 978-0-9831268-2-9 (paper)
ISBN 978-0-9831268-3-6 (electronic)

Library of Congress Control Number: 2011941257

Printed in the United States of America

Books by Michael Lee Lanning

The Only War We Had: A Platoon Leader's Journal of Vietnam

Vietnam 1969-1970: A Company Commander's Journal

Inside the LRRPs: Rangers in Vietnam

Inside Force Recon: Recon Marines in Vietnam (with Ray W. Stubbe)

The Battles of Peace

Inside the VC and NVA: The Real Story of North Vietnam's Armed Forces (with Dan Cragg)

Vietnam at the Movies

Senseless Secrets: The Failures of U. S. Military Intelligence From George Washington to the Present

The Military 100: A Ranking of the Most Influential Military Leaders of All Time

The African-American Soldier: From Crispus Attucks to Colin Powell

Inside the Crosshairs: Snipers in Vietnam

Defenders of Liberty: African-Americans in the Revolutionary War

Blood Warriors: American Military Elites.

The Battle 100: The Stories Behind History's Most Influential Battles

Mercenaries: Soldiers of Fortune, From Ancient Greece to Today's Private Military Companies

The Civil War 100: The Stories Behind the Most Influential Battles, People, and Events in the War Between the States

The Revolutionary War 100: The People, Battles, and Events of the American War for Independence, Ranked by their Significance

Dedication:

To truth, justice, honor, honesty, courage, loyalty, and fairness. Characteristics often absent in the events behind the following story.

Contents

Introduction

When approached by my publisher about writing this book, I had mixed emotions—a sparked interest and a skeptical apprehension among them—concerning whether or not the topic and I were right for each other. I do watch the occasional football game on television, but I have not attended a college matchup in years. I keep up with the Top 25 polls through the sports section in the daily newspaper, but I do so more to be informed than because I am a great fan of college football.

I was aware that Texas Tech University fired Mike Leach, mostly because the timing of his surprise termination made the regular news as well as sports headlines. Although I had no "dog in the hunt"—or more aptly "no player on the field"—the story was of interest since I had grown up near Lubbock, had myself attended the Red Raiders' rival Texas A&M University, and have a daughter who is a Tech graduate. Residing in Phoenix, Arizona near the publisher at the time of his inquiry, I felt fairly removed from the details surrounding the controversial dismissal; however, my wife and I were rebuilding our home on the Bolivar Peninsula on the Texas Gulf Coast that we had lost to Hurricane Ike in 2008, and soon I would be much nearer the primary players in this deepening drama. For all these reasons, I was certainly intrigued by the book's topic.

As a researcher, writer, and historian, I have previously written military history with a focus on the Vietnam War era. My other books chronicle battles and leaders as far back as 3000 BC. But after turning to my computer and making a brief initial search on the phrase "Mike Leach Texas Tech," I quickly discovered that an incident as recent as two years ago—and continuing today— is much easier in most ways to investigate but more difficult in others than incidents that occurred decades or even centuries ago. The good news and bad news are the same—information is everywhere. Basic internet searches simply overwhelm.

Yet sources on this particular subject crossed all genre lines, conflicted grossly, or simply made no sense. The more I read, the more it appeared that writers of many articles had more interest in agendas than in facts. Accounts of the same issue were often as radically different as political stories produced by the Fox News Channel and MSNBC.

As research progressed, I quickly discovered the Leach supporters to be more available and forthright than the Texas Tech University administrators, who seemed to have adopted a deep-bunker mentality. It soon became apparent that something was just not right—morally or legally. From the outset, the firing of Mike Leach appeared to be more the result of the good old boy buddy system at work than any sound business practice in play, more about personal politics for control than basic professionalism, and more about finances than fairness. But I wanted to gather all the evidence and details in order to present a fair analysis.

I have made every effort in this book to cover both sides of the controversy. I have cited court documents, depositions, and personal interviews that have been at the forefront of my research as well as opinion columns, internet blogs, and other commentary available. The conclusions reached in this book are my own—based on the facts as I understand them. All readers are, of course, entitled to make up their own minds.

Michael Lee Lanning
Bolivar Peninsula, Texas
October 2011

Chapter 1

On the Sidelines:
The Firing of Mike Leach

Mike Leach sat on the sidelines. Not in San Antonio's Alamodome preparing his Texas Tech University Red Raiders for the 2010 Alamo Bowl against the Michigan State Spartans as he had expected. Instead he was alone in his hotel room. Instead of working on plans for the game scheduled for January 2, Leach was awaiting a legal decision from the 99th Judicial Court in Lubbock, a ruling that would either lift or uphold his coaching suspension imposed two days before by his bosses, Texas Tech Athletic Director Gerald Myers and University President Guy Bailey. (Organizational Authority for Texas Tech Administrators and Board of Regents at Appendix A.)

Leach and the Red Raiders had departed Lubbock in high spirits for San Antonio on Monday, December 28, 2009 to complete preparations for the upcoming post-season bowl game to be played four days later. The team—after its spectacular 2008 year—had just completed another successful season, racking up an 8-4 record and making Mike Leach the most winning football coach in Texas Tech history. Not only had the Red Raiders, who had been un-ranked and mostly unnoted a decade before Leach took over, gained national recognition, but also they had done it in a style that old-school proponents of the game said could not be done. Coach Leach had had the vision, and his players had executed it right into the Top 25 in the polls. The Raiders had been flying in more ways than just on planes.

Upon his arrival in the Alamo City, however, Leach received a stunning telephone call from Athletic Director Myers telling him that he had been suspended from coaching duties—effective immediately—until further notice.

Leach was shocked. Here he was at the pinnacle of his coaching career at a major bowl game with an opportunity for him and his team to gain even more national attention and to move up in the Top 25 polls. The previous year's team had elevated Tech as high as number 2 in the country; the Alamo Bowl, while not a top tier contest, would validate that the Red Raiders had become a national powerhouse and that their radically different style of offense was changing the face of modern football.

Now instead of euphoria and a cheering crowd, Leach stood alone against the forces of incredible accusations and an entrenched university administration and Board of Regents. In weather, it would have been called the perfect storm; in football terms, Leach now faced the perfect blitz. From one side of the field of perspectives and agenda, the attacks were coming fast and furiously from an ESPN sports commentator who was using a microphone from his on-air bully pulpit to accuse Leach of abusing his son. Part of the reason that the suspension caught Leach off-guard was that he thought the complaint issue had been resolved, having been told by the university's attorney-investigator just days before that she had finished her inquiries and that there was nothing for him to worry about—not that he was overly concerned since he believed he had done nothing wrong in regard to his player. Nevertheless, he had been glad to have the incident behind him so that he could concentrate on the bowl game with no distractions. Or so he had thought.

But the moves against Leach were not that simple or singular. From another, unexpected side of events, the threats were mounting from what looked like thwarted, hostile Board of Regents members who could now see their way to finally out-maneuver Leach, take him down, and save themselves a bundle of cash—all that the same time. When they saw Leach weakened by very public and unanswered accusations, they appeared to have recognized an opportunity for revenge and for saving the university some cash.

Leach, however, was not on the field of play alone. He had dozens of happy players and thousands of jubilant fans at his back; and a staff of loyal coaches and trainers to his front. In the end, however, none of the defenses or supporters could do anything to stop the assault on his reputation and character.

As a part of the brief conversation suspending him from his job, Athletic Director Myers read Leach the letter written on Office of the President stationary: "Dear Coach Leach: We recently received a complaint from a player and his parents regarding your treatment of him after an injury, and we have undertaken an investigation of that complaint. We consider this a serious matter. Until the investigation is complete, you are suspended from all duties as Head Football Coach effective immediately."

Though surprised, disappointed, and hurt, Leach did not hang his head. He did what he had done all his life when faced with adversity: the Coach fought back. Less than twenty-four hours later, Leach directed his attorney, Ted Liggett of Lubbock, to file a temporary restraining order (TRO) against the suspension based on the failure of Texas Tech to follow due process and for breach of the coach's contract. The District Court, recognizing the time sensitivity of the matter, had set a hearing for 10:00 a.m. on Wednesday, December 30, just three days before the big game.

Because Leach was still in San Antonio, his attorney Liggett approached the courthouse without his client on that Wednesday morning of the 30th , bundled against a driving wind that had brought a light dusting of fresh snow the day before. Stomping through even deeper slush and ice left from a powerful winter storm that had hit the Plains less than a week earlier, the lawyer entered the building only to find an atmosphere even colder than the one outside

Liggett had prepared for a hearing with the presiding judge over the TRO issue and had intended to proceed straight to the judge's chambers. Instead, outside the judge's office, he encountered the attorney representing Texas Tech University who informed him that if he proceeded with the hearing on the temporary restraining order, Leach would immediately be terminated as the football coach and as an employee of Texas Tech. Liggett responded that he did indeed intend to proceed, to which the Tech counsel made no comment but rather reached into his briefcase and handed Liggett a letter from his client. In fewer than three dozen words, Texas Tech University President Guy Bailey fired Leach: "This letter shall serve as a formal notice to you that, pursuant to Article V of your Employment Contract, you are terminated with cause effective immediately, for breach of the provisions of Article IV of that Contract." (Contract at Appendix B.)

Liggett called Leach with the news and then met with reporters and the public who were still in the courthouse expecting the now-canceled hearing to begin. After Liggett read the termination letter, the crowd reacted in disbelief, one man yelling, "You can stuff my season tickets!"

The news swept from Lubbock to San Antonio and rippled across the country—and indeed, the world—in minutes via sports radio and television, blogs, and other media outlets. The story that a university would fire its most successful coach ever on the eve of a nationally televised bowl game was so baffling that it quickly leaped from the sports sections to national news headlines.

Questions came from all directions: Why would Tech fire the coach with the most football wins in its history, a mentor who had one of the highest percentages of graduating players in the NCAA, and an individual who had brought national attention and significant additional revenues to Texas Tech and its football program?

The Texas Tech administration immediately went on the offensive to justify what was quickly becoming a very unpopular decision on their part. Shortly after the news broke, Tech issued a statement that read in part, "After reviewing all the information available, Texas Tech University has decided that the best course of action for the university and football program is to terminate its relationship with Head Football Coach Mike Leach for cause."

The statement continued, "The coach's termination was precipitated by his treatment of a player after the player was diagnosed with a concussion. The player was put at risk for additional injury. After the university was apprised of the treatment, Coach Leach was contacted by the administration of the university in an attempt to resolve the problem. In a defiant act of insubordination, Coach Leach continually refused to cooperate in a meaningful way to help resolve the complaint…. This action, along with his continuous acts of insubordination, resulted in irreconcilable differences that make it impossible for Coach Leach to remain at Texas Tech." (Complete statement at Appendix C)

Texas Tech University System Board of Regents Chairman Larry Anders and Vice Chairman Jerry Turner voiced their support for the termination. Both lauded the "leadership" Athletic Director Myers and University President Bailey had exhibited in taking the action. University Chancellor Kent Hance told the Lubbock *Avalanche-Journal,* "This is sad. The only person responsible for Mike Leach being gone is Mike Leach."

Those who were following Tech football and ESPN television already knew that the episode, at least on the surface, involved the alleged mistreatment of sophomore player Adam James, son of former Southern Methodist University and National Football League star Craig James. The elder James, an on-camera ESPN personality, analyst, and sports announcer—scheduled to be an on-air commentator for the Alamo Bowl—had already been broadcasting his belief that his son had been mistreated by Coach Leach. There can be little doubt that pressure from national exposure for employing and tolerating an allegedly abusive coach, as James presented Leach in his son's side of the story, influenced Tech officials. Or, did it simply hand them an excuse they had been waiting for?

The James family announced on December 30, "We appreciate that the University conducted a fair and thorough investigation." Even though the statement added that there would be no further comment at that time, Craig James was right back on ESPN voicing his view of the situation, giving interviews, and answering questions as they came to him. On December 19—just two days after his son's first alleged mistreatment and more than a week before Leach was suspended—James the elder had already hired his own public relations firm to assist him in publicly presenting his son's claims. Some sources point to James hiring the PR firm as much as ten days earlier.

The basis of the James family outrage was that Adam had supposedly been endangered when the coach failed to appropriately respond to his concussion. The evidence that Craig James presented to the world was a 16-second, jerkily amateurish cell phone video shot on December 19 showing Adam allegedly confined in an "electrical closet" while the rest of the team practiced for the Alamo Bowl. However, the hair-trigger first response to activate a public relations firm rather than rush his son to a doctor indicates that the James complaint was much more about Adam's lack of playing time and star treatment than about Adam's "playing" time in an electrical closet.

Once news of Leach's termination reached national headlines, rumors and theories began to surface that exposed the lingering and festering hostilities that had existed between Leach and the university since negotiations over his 2008 contract. Or perhaps more accurately stated, lingering and festering feelings of hostility apparently held by some of the members of the Board of Regents toward Leach as a result of the outcome of those negotiations. The fact that Tech saved $800,000 by firing Leach when they did—money that would have been due him as a bonus negotiated in that contract—did not escape notice or suspicion.

A still-stunned Mike Leach packed his bags in San Antonio and turned the team over to assistant Ruffin McNeill. In a statement to the news media Leach said, "I want everyone to know what a privilege and pleasure it has been to teach and coach more than 400 student-athletes at Texas Tech University."

But Leach was not going away quietly. After noting the accomplishments of his decade at Tech, he continued, "Over the past several months, there have been individuals in the Texas Tech administration, Board of Regents, and booster groups who have dealt in lies, and continue to do so. These lies have led to my firing this morning. I steadfastly refuse to deal in any lies, and am disappointed that I have not been afforded the opportunity for the truth to be known. Texas Tech's decision to deal in lies and fabricate a story which led to my firing, includes, but is not limited by, animosity from last year's contract negotiations. I will not tolerate such retaliatory action; additionally, we will pursue all available legal remedies."

In summary Leach stated, "These actions taken by Texas Tech have severely damaged my reputation and public image. In addition, Texas Tech has caused harm not only to my family, but to the entire Red Raider Nation and the sport of college football." (Complete statement at Appendix D.)

Leach was especially on target about the Red Raider Nation. Tech boosters and alumni—who had been thrilled to watch their team soar into high-scoring victories for almost a decade— flooded the blogs and Letters to the Editors columns, supporting the coach more than ten to one. A common thread bound their complaints: the Double T had double crossed their favorite coach.

Chapter 2

Mike Leach: The Early Years

As a boy and as a young man growing up, Mike Leach had no plans to become a football coach. But when he set his mind to the task as an adult, he rose to the ranks of the most successful and innovative leaders on the gridiron. His teams set records; his players won awards. He broke all the old rules, and then put the game back together in an extraordinarily new way.

Leach was born on March 9, 1961 in the northern California town of Susanville, but his family moved often before eventually settling in Cody, Wyoming near Yellowstone National Park when Leach was a young boy. In Cody he went out for the high school football team but spent most of his time on the bench as a reserve. While Leach was not much of a player, he was an intense observer and student of the game.

Upon graduation, Leach, raised as a member of The Church of Jesus Christ of Latter Day Saints, enrolled in Brigham Young University where he participated in rugby matches. He played no football in Provo but he did continue his observations of the game as he closely followed the BYU Cougars football team with its spread-out, pass-oriented offense under head coach LaVell Edwards and offensive coordinator Norm Chow.

After his graduation in 1983, Leach enrolled in the law school at Pepperdine University in California where he became enamored with the ocean and the beach, both of which would remain more fascinating and inspiring to him than the law. By the time he graduated, Leach was doubting his decision to become an attorney. Despite having a wife and one child to support, he decided he definitely did not want to practice law. Instead, he proclaimed that what he really wanted to become was a football coach, and he enrolled in the United States Sports Academy in Daphne, Alabama—the first, only, and likely last

Doctor of Jurisprudence graduate of Pepperdine University School of Law to do so.

Leach completed the USSA program only to find that job openings in the upper levels of the coaching profession were few, especially for a man with no experience playing college football. In 1987, he lobbied his way into a position as assistant coach of safeties and offensive linemen at Cal Poly at San Luis Obispo, a Division II school.

The satisfaction was enormous, but the monetary rewards were small. When Leach told his wife Sharon that he would be earning $3,000, she assumed that they could live on that monthly income. When he explained that the amount was for the whole year, Sharon reached for the want ads. She found a job as an administrative assistant in a local vineyard, and Mike did odd jobs, such as substitute teaching, to supplement their income.

A year later the Leaches moved inland to the College of the Desert in Palm Desert, California, where he would coach linebackers. Although it was a step down from a Division II school to a junior college, his salary rose to an annual sum of $12,000. Sharon found another job, this time as an admin assistant on the campus.

In early 1989, Leach accepted the head coach position of the Poli Bears, a professional European football league in Finland. His stay with the Finns was brief, not because the players smoked cigarettes on the beach during games but because of a better offer back in the States.

The fall of 1989 found Leach in Mount Pleasant, Iowa, as the offensive line coach at Wesleyan College, a National Association of Intercollegiate Athletics (NAIA) school with fewer than a thousand students. While the institution had neither a strong football tradition nor a winning record, it was a four-year school, and more important, the head coach was Hal Mumme, a man who would mentor and mold Leach into a powerful purveyor of a new type of football.

At first glance, Mumme would not leap out of coaching history as one to be such an inspiration and role model. Following an unsuccessful stint as the offensive coordinator at the University of Texas at El Paso from 1982-1985, Mumme accepted the head coach position at Copperas Cove High School in Central Texas. There Mumme adopted techniques he had seen be successful for LaVell Edwards at BYU. He instituted a spread-out, pass-oriented, multiple-receiver offense. This strategy, combined with tough players from military families stationed at nearby Fort Hood, began to defeat Texas powerhouse schools that had previously dominated the region.

When Mumme moved up to Iowa Wesleyan, Leach was one of the first assistants he hired. In an article by S. C. Gwynne in the September 2009 edition of *Texas Monthly Magazine,* Leach—when asked why Mumme had chosen him—explained, "He probably thought I was ambitious and would do anything he told me. He was right."

In the spring of 1989, Mumme and Leach attended the BYU training camp and then leap-frogged across the country visiting other pass-oriented programs. By the time they returned to Iowa, they had formulated the basics for their offense, which would be operating primarily out of the shotgun formation and throwing the ball to multiple receivers. Instead of a ball-control and time-of-possession approach, they focused on speed and simplicity. In the same interview with *Texas Monthly,* Mumme recalled, "We just saw time differently than other coaches did. You can replace personnel. You can replace equipment. Time is the only thing you can't replace in a game. So we wanted to run as many plays as we could in the time allowed."

The innovative offense worked. Wesleyan's football record was 0 and 10 before Mumme and Leach. Over the next three years, the coaches added a no-huddle scheme to their offense and won 25 while losing only 10 as they set 26 national NAIA records. Along with the wins and records came rewards for Leach, small though they may have been. His starting salary of $13,000 rose to $22,000. Despite his meager wages, Leach was happy doing what he wanted to do.

The advancement of football coaches follows a simple route.

Win and move up. In 1992, Mumme and Leach did just that when they went to Division II Valdosta State in Georgia. Valdosta State was another school with a long-standing losing record. Over the next five years, the Mumme-Leach duo led the college to 40 wins versus 17 losses and a single tie as they consistently ranked in the Top 20 of Division II schools and set 35 conference records and 7 national benchmarks. During this time Leach continued developing his skills in coaching quarterbacks, culminating in his signal caller Chris Hatcher's earning the Division II Player of the Year title.

In 1997 Mumme landed a new job, and did not hesitate to take Leach with him as his offensive coordinator. Their successes continued at the University of Kentucky with what quickly was dubbed the "Air Raid Offense." In two years the team set 41 Southeast Conference records as Leach implemented his quarterback development methods. During Leach's second year as offensive coordinator, UK quarterback Tim Couch completed passes for 4,275 yards, earning honors as first team All American, Heisman Trophy finalist, and the number one pick in the NFL draft.

In 1999 Leach left Mumme and UK to join the newly hired Bob Stoops at the University of Oklahoma. The once-famed Oklahoma program had fallen on hard times and Stoops realized that major changes had to take place to return the program to national prominence. One such change was to give Leach the leeway to convert the run-dominated offense to a pass-oriented attack. Leach relished the challenge though he was not satisfied with the OU quarterbacks who had been recruited to direct a running offense. Leach went looking for a new signal caller. He found his man, Josh Heupel, at remote Snow College in Utah. When Leach offered him a spot at OU, Heupel was playing only about half the time at Snow.

Oklahoma fans were not happy with Leach, his new passing offense, or the quarterback he recruited to run it. Leach recalled the situation, saying, "There was a time when the two most wanted people in the state were me and Josh Heupel. I was the guy who thought we were going to throw the ball. Heupel was the quarterback who couldn't run."

Supporters jumped on board the Stoops/Leach bandwagon when the team won 7 games and lost only 5, an improvement from the 5 and 6 season of 1998. More important, and certainly more entertaining for the fans, was the increase from the previous year's average of 16.7 points per game to an average 36.8 per contest.

In 2000, Oklahoma went 13-0, winning the national championship. Heupel earned honors as the Heisman Trophy runner-up. Leach, however, was not around for the victory celebrations. He had finally achieved his goal. Leach, at age 38, was about to assume his first role as head coach with his hiring by Texas Tech University.

Chapter 3

On the Plains: "Happiness is Lubbock, Texas..."

Mike Leach was ready for Texas Tech. Since college football fields measure the same regardless of the campus and the game's rules are standard, Leach felt confident he could recruit players for the Red Raiders who could execute his plans. Whether or not Lubbock was ready for Mike Leach was another question.

In a May 3, 2011 article in the *New York Times*, reporter Randy Kennedy described Lubbock, writing, "...this small city on the tableland of the Southern Great Plains has never had a lot to recommend it, culturally or aesthetically.'"

A regional center for commerce, medical facilities, and education, Lubbock has garnered prominence not so much for its resources as for its central location on the "tableland." The city has become the 11th largest in the state and the hub of activity serving the vast region that separates it from other metropolises. Dallas is 340 miles southeast while El Paso is equidistance to the southwest; Austin, the state capital, sits 400 miles away; Houston, the state's largest city, is 524 miles southeast. Albuquerque, New Mexico and Oklahoma City, Oklahoma are closer than most of the Texas cities, each about 350 miles away.

Today's city of Lubbock did not exist, however, until 1890 and then only because it merged with Monterey, another village across the canyon. The citizens of the two settlements agreed to join forces by keeping the Monterey location but renaming it Lubbock. The townspeople of "old Lubbock" moved their homes and businesses, to the combined town site. A year later Lubbock became the official county seat of Lubbock County; the city incorporated on March 16, 1909.

Texas Technological College, forerunner of Texas Tech

University, was established in 1923 and for more than a quarter century remained the town's most widely known entity. In the latter half of the 20th century, the surrounding Lubbock area began developing into what has become the largest contiguous cotton-growing region in the world, supported by irrigation water from the Ogallala Aquifer as the area receives only an average of 18.7 inches of rainfall and 10.2 inches of snowfall annually.

For its size and age, Lubbock has produced remarkably few famous natives and the two best known came out of the music industry. Scott "Mac" Davis, a popular country and western, rock crossover artist, song writer and actor, was born in Lubbock on January 21, 1942. The Academy of Country Music named Davis *Entertainer of the Year* for 1974. Interestingly, his most widely known song is *Happiness is Texas in My Rearview Mirror* that contains the more notable line, *I thought happiness was Lubbock, Texas in my rearview mirror."*

Undoubtedly the most famous son of Lubbock is pioneer rock-and-roller Buddy Holly. Born Charles Hardin Holley on September 7, 1936, he changed the spelling of his name and wrote his own songs as Buddy Holly. He established the standard composition for future rock bands: two guitars, a base, and drums.

Holly signed his first professional music contract with Decca Records in early 1957 and recorded hit after hit with his band the Crickets before his death in an airplane crash near Clear Lake, Iowa, on February 3, 1959. The Beatles later said that Holly had a great influence on their music, including giving their own group another insect name in recognition of the Crickets. Bob Dylan, the Rolling Stones, Eric Clapton, Elton John, and the Grateful Dead also recorded Holly's songs and paid homage to his lasting influence.

Six months before his death, Holly met Maria Elena Santiago, a receptionist for a publisher in New York, to whom he proposed on their first date. On August 15, 1958 the couple flew to Lubbock for the wedding, Maria Elena's first and only visit to the city on the plains. She did not attend Buddy's funeral in Lubbock; she has never visited his grave. But, as the owner of the rights to Holly's name and songs, she charged the City of Lubbock $20,000 for a twenty-year license to maintain the name on its Buddy Holly Center.

Holly rests today under a modest marker that simply reads, "In Loving Memory of Our Son," recording his name as Buddy Holley, his dates of birth and death, and a carving of his Fender Stratocaster guitar.

Despite his fame, Lubbock itself did not really accept Holly as an honored native until many years after his death. Lubbock was and is not a rock-and-roll town. It is a city of churches and church-goers. Within the city limits are 68 Baptist, 27 Church of Christ, 24 Methodists and 18 Catholic churches. Another 80 houses of worship of various dominations dot the city, mostly Protestant but with one Muslim mosque, and one each Hindu and Jewish temple. A single LDS temple also joins the list.

While most of the various religions represented in Lubbock get along, at least on the surface, there are some deep-seated beliefs in West Texas and on the Plains that meet or perhaps exceed those of other regions. The Baptists think the Methodists are much too liberal, neither can understand why the Church of Christ does not allow a piano to accompany their hymns, and all three consider the Catholic Church as necessary for Hispanics (who make up nearly a fourth of the local population), out-of-state Tech students, and emigrant Yankees. Not even considering the Jews, Hindus, Muslims, and Mormons, each religion is pretty sure that the believers of all the others are going to burn in hell anyway.

Many in Lubbock in the 1950s considered the joining of Buddy Holly and Maria Elena Santiago to be a mixed marriage. There are still some today who consider spouses from different religious affiliations should carry the same moniker. A woman who grew up in a small town near Lubbock recalls, "My grandparents had a mixed marriage. She a Baptist, he Church of Christ. They were married for more than sixty years but every

Sunday she would go to her church, he to his."

Regardless of their religious differences and other various distinguishing features, the people of Lubbock are generally hard-working, fair, and honest in a way that reflects the continuing pioneer spirit of the region. They represent hardy stock who survive the difficult challenges that the land and weather provide. Cowboy hats, boots, and western wear remain as common as suits and ties in the Lubbock business district. A handshake on a deal remains as good as a signed, notarized, contract.

Texas Tech, like any other university, is very much a city within itself. Established on February 10, 1923, Tech boasts a campus of 1,839 acres (nearly three square miles), the second largest contiguous campus in the United States, where students can study for undergraduate and post-graduate, law, and medical degrees at the same location. Author James Mitchener once described the Spanish Renaissance-style campus as "the most beautiful west of the Mississippi until you get to Stanford." In 2008 Stewart Mandel in *Sports Illustrated* described Tech as "easily one of ten most beautiful campuses" in the country.

With more than 31,000 students, Tech today ranks as the seventh largest university in Texas. Although Tech enrolls students from all 50 states and from more than a hundred foreign countries, the vast majority are natives of, and share basic values with, West Texas. The University has been somewhat more successful than Lubbock in producing noteworthy alumni. Its most prominent political graduates include the president of Panama from 1969-1978, Demetrio B. Lakas, and three state governors: Preston Smith of Texas in 1968-1972, Daniel Thornton of Colorado from 1951-1955, and John Burroughs of New Mexico from 1959-1961.

Four NASA astronauts are also Tech graduates as is the first Hispanic U.S. Army four star general, Richard E. Cavazos. Four Red Raiders have risen to head major U.S. companies, including General Motors and the Belo Corporation. Singer John Denver was a Tech alumni. On the more notorious side, John Hinckley, Jr., who attempted to assassinate President Ronald Reagan in 1981, enrolled in the university off and on from 1973 to 1980.

Texas Tech athletic teams participated in the Border Intercollegiate Athletic Conference from 1932 to 1956. After more than twenty years of lobbying and eight rejections, Tech was finally permitted to join the Southwest Conference in 1956. When the SWC disbanded in 1995, Tech, along with the University of Texas, Baylor, and Texas A&M merged with the Big 8 to form the Big 12.

In its long sports history Tech has managed but one national championship. In 1993, the Lady Raiders basketball team, led by Sheryl Swoops, claimed the national title.

The most widely recognized symbol of Texas Tech University is its Double T icon that is generally thought to have originated with E. Y. Freeland, Tech's head football coach from 1925 to1928. Although its original red, black, and white block configuration has been slightly modified over the years, the Double T remains the icon of the university.

Co-existing on the vast West Texas Plains, where cultural amenities struggle and the gridiron is king, both Tech and Lubbock have come to hold some definite ideas about what to expect from their football coaches. Throughout the state, many fans claim that in Texas there are only two sports—football and spring practice.

In the fall on Friday nights, entire towns empty into their local stadiums or journey hundreds of miles to fill the visitors' bleachers to watch their high school players. On Saturdays they cheer their favorite Texas college team, which in the Lubbock region is Tech and no other.

At every level in almost every town and city, the football coach is not only the leader of the team but also a spokesman and representative of the community. His influence often exceeds that of local politicians and clergymen. Coaches play golf with the fans—especially donors to their program—speak at local civic and booster events, and endure being either heralded or vilified in the sports pages and on street corners depending on their wins and losses.

Into these expectations and traditions rode individualistic Mike Leach, arriving at Tech to find the administration, faculty, and the townspeople assuming he would continue down the same "good old boy" path of his predecessor. Spike Dykes, who had coached at Tech since 1984, was born in the shadows of Tech's Jones Stadium in 1938 as the son of a cotton ginner.

Dykes fit in well with the Tech administrators and regents, most of whom are also originally from Lubbock and many of whom had played college football. He shared their basic beliefs and values, spoke their language, and, more importantly, showed proper deference to his superiors and actively courted high-roller donors. During his tenure of more than a dozen years, Dykes managed to win enough games (82-67-1) to keep most of the administration and fans reasonably happy. His teams finished in the national Top 20 only twice and never broke into the Top 10, but Dykes' longevity earned him the title as the winningest football coach in Tech history at the time. Dykes completed the 1999 season with a 6-5 record.

Well aware that the Red Raider Nation had tired of his inability to break out of the ranks of mediocrity, he announced his retirement after the season's final game. Many observers believe that Dykes resigned to keep from being fired. Several of the same Tech administrators and board members who later went after Mike Leach's job were also thought to be behind the exit of Dykes.

Chapter 4

Head Coach Mike Leach: Early and Sustained Success, 2000-2007

Assistant football coaches rarely come to the attention of the media. So it was with Mike Leach for the first dozen years of his career when only the most hardcore fans knew he existed. That was to change when he arrived at Texas Tech and Lubbock on December 9, 1999. Instead of being a footnote to the careers of head coaches Mumme and Stoops, Leach would for the next ten years draw the attention not only of the local media but also of the state and national outlets.

The anticipation of Leach's taking over as the head coach of the Red Raiders was a two-way street. Leach was eager to prove his football philosophy would win; the Raider fans were eager to embrace their new leader who, they hoped, would take them to victories and national prominence.

The people of Lubbock did not know how to take Leach when he first came to town. He did not dress like a football coach. He wore beach shorts and sandals, not sweat suits and a whistle. He did not golf with the university staff and donors. He was more likely to go rollerblading or read a good book. He did not talk like a football coach. Instead of going into deep details about a play or a game plan to show how "football smart" he was—which everyone was interested in hearing—he would start a discussion of world events or history. Some of the good church-goers of Lubbock also murmured about his Mormon background.

When asked if he thought living in Lubbock would be a cultural shock after growing up in Wyoming, Leach responded in his stream-of-conscious manner, "I don't think so. The people are incredibly similar. They're friendly people here. The weather's nicer here. The mountains are shorter here."

Leach was not the good old boy West Texan that the Red Raider Nation had grown used to. Some thought his behavior to be just plain strange. A number of Tech administrators found him standoffish and not nearly as acquiescing as his predecessors. They later claimed he should have done more to solicit contributions from former students and supporters, but, in fact, Leach went on 65 stops to speak to boosters in his first year alone at Tech and accepted virtually every offer to appear at fundraisers.

While school officials kept their concerns to themselves, the people of Lubbock were more vocal about the new coach. Skip Watson, retired news director of KCBD-TV and former director of public information for the Lubbock Independent School District explains, "Lubbock is a big city of more than 200,000, but in many ways it is still a small town. Everyone is careful about what they say today as they never know who they will be doing business with tomorrow. Lubbock is a quiet, careful place.

"But, they still gossip," Watson continued in an April 2011 interview, "especially about newcomers. When Leach first got here things kind of started slow. Then rumors began that he drank and ran around but I never heard anything to back up any of these claims. These stories stopped as he began to win games and soon everyone was talking about what a great family man he was."

Leach, despite inheriting mismatched players from the Dykes years, immediately began to win ball games. In 2000, his first season in Lubbock, Tech went 7-6 and earned an invitation to the galleryfurniture.com Bowl in Houston. Over the next seven seasons Tech averaged more than eight victories annually and played in a bowl game each year. This record is all that more remarkable in that Tech played in the highly competitive Big 12 Conference with yearly games against Texas, Oklahoma, and Texas A&M.

By 2004 Tech had broken into the National Top 25 rankings where it would remain for much of the next five years. Leach's Red Raiders continually ranked at or near the top in national total offense and scoring. He also continued his success in developing quarterbacks with Tech signal callers breaking Big 12 and national passing records.

A student and master of the game of football, Leach does not, however, limit his life to the gridiron. His interests range far and wide. Most coaches talk endlessly about Xs and Os, past games, future contests, and recruiting prospects. Those who reach the top levels of the profession combine intelligence, instinct, and occasionally ruthlessness to win games and keep their jobs. Even so, few coaches at any level are stamped as intellectuals. A Renaissance Man among the coaching ranks is rare indeed.

Mike Leach is not the typical coach. People close to him say that he is usually "the smartest guy in the room." Others expand that to "smartest in the whole damn building." As one of the only coaches in the upper legions of football with a law degree, Leach possesses an insatiable curiosity about the unknown and an intense drive to learn new things. He is the only major football coach to publish an article in a law school review. In comparing the relationship between coaching football and practicing law in the *Texas Tech Law Review,* he wrote, "Both law school and college football view it as important to harden and battle test your charges the best you can before you turn them out into the real world."

Leach's interests, both intellectual and fanciful, extend far beyond his professional fields. Each off-season Leach immerses himself in one or more new subjects. Past topics have included those related to his love of the beach such as studying the effects of offshore wave breaks on the Southern California coast, whales, and sharks. He has also delved into the lives of pioneers and Old West characters such as Daniel Boone, Wyatt Earp, and Doc Holliday. He also concentrated on chimpanzees and grizzly bears. Leach recognizes many similarities between football and warfare, having extensively studied World War II, the American Civil War, the culture and history of the Vikings, Winston Churchill, and Napoleon Bonaparte. In his quest for knowledge and understanding, Leach has researched subjects as wide-ranging as from the continent of Australia and the artist Jackson Pollock to the assassination of John F. Kennedy. Pictures and mementos of his studies covered the wall of his office at Texas Tech, including the original death certificate of Apache leader Geronimo, another focus of the coach's interests.

Of all his quests for information, none have had more impact on Leach's philosophy of life and football than his fascination with pirates. He encouraged each of his players to "swing your sword" while he moved a six-foot motion-activated buccaneer skeleton into his office. The concept of pirates and Red Raiders seemed to go hand-in-hand.

Actually, Leach did not introduce the pirate theme to his team until 2003 when they lost for a second straight year to Missouri, putting them at 5-3 for the season. The day after the latest defeat at the team meeting, Leach brought in a sword, swung it around the room, and lectured his players on the diversity, organization, and work ethics of pirates. He told them they should prepare their bodies for football the way pirates hone their swords for battle. The players—and then the student body and next the fans and finally the media—picked up on the pirate theme. Skull and cross-bone flags began to appear in the stadiums, as did eye patches and swords.

In an interview with Mark Schlabach of ESPN Television on May 7, 2008, Leach explained, "Pirates function as a team. There were a lot of castes and classes in England at the time. But with pirates, it didn't matter if you were black, white, rich or poor. The object was to get a treasure. If the captain did a bad job, you just throw him overboard."

Some say that Mike Leach marches to a different drummer—or more precisely, to a whole different band.

When Scott Pelley—a Tech alumni himself—interviewed Leach on CBS's *60 Minutes* in late 2008, he baited the coach by saying, "One sportswriter called you a 'football madman' directing a sideshow."

The coach responded, "Yeah, well, I don't have any disagreement with it really."

Mike Leach's winning formula is actually amazingly simplistic. He recruits the smartest, fastest players available and places them in relatively few formations with multiple options. He has no play book as such and relies on repetition, repetition, repetition in practice so the players are precise and confident on each down. In every facet of training Leach is deeply involved. He stays on top of every situation, following his mantra, "You are either coaching it, or you are allowing it to happen."

Oddly the Tech offense never developed a catchy moniker, at least none that stuck. Fans and sports writers alike came to refer to the methodology as "Mike's" or "Tech's offense."

Most collegiate teams' passing formations include only three receivers, but on nearly every play Leach sends five, and he claims he would send more if the game rules allowed. This requires the defensive units to protect the entire field from sideline to sideline and from line of scrimmage to the goal line on every play.

Michael Lewis, writing in the *New York Times* on December 4, 2005, explained, "Stretching out the offensive line stretched out the defensive line too, forcing the most ferocious pass rushers several yards farther from the quarterback. It also opened up wide passing lanes through which even a short quarterback could see the whole field clearly. Leach spread out his receivers and backs too. The look was more flag football: a truly fantastic number of players racing around trying to catch passes on every play, and a quarterback surprisingly able to keep an eye on all of them."

Along with using the entire field, Leach believes in speeding up the game with constant attack. Where most offenses run between 65 and 70 plays a game, Leach's offense averages 85 to 90. As one of the few head coaches who also acts as his own offensive coordinator, he signals the plays to his un-huddled offense. He is not, however, inflexible in his play-calling. He gives his quarterback full authority to change the play regardless of the down or line of scrimmage. In the article by Lewis, Leach explained, "He can see more than I'll ever see. If I call a stupid play, his job is to get me out of it. If he doesn't get me out of it,

I might holler at him. But if you let him react to what he sees, there's a ton of touchdowns to be had."

And indeed a "ton of touchdowns" were had by the Tech team under Leach's tutelage. The teams typically put over 40 points on the scoreboard each game and on occasion as many as 70. In 2004, Tech scored that 70-point high against TCU and then again the same number against Nebraska, the most the Cornhuskers had given up in their 114 years of playing football. The following year the Red Raiders scored 158 total points in a three-game run against teams ranked first, eighth, and nineteenth in the country.

Leach disdains having his team punt the ball and settle for field goals; he loves the spread-and-pass-offense. He will go for a first down on fourth and multiple yards rather than kick the ball away regardless of field position. He figures that if he is unsuccessful he will get the ball back eventually and once again march down for another score. Leach's players understand the philosophy but still marvel at the approach. Cody Hodges, who sat on the sidelines learning the system before becoming a starter, recalled, according to the article by Lewis, "There's been lots of times I'm on the sidelines, and I'm like, 'Oh God, we're going for it!' We went for it on fourth and 5 on our own 23—in the first quarter. We went for it once on fourth and 18—and we were ahead."

In the same article another member of the 2005 team explained the "go for it" practice a bit more philosophically. Offensive lineman E. J. Whitley stated, "If you're on this offense, you expect to score. Most offenses on fourth down are coming off the field. On fourth down we expect a play to be called. Because we haven't scored yet."

Leach's defenses are more traditional yet still simplistic. At Tech he had his players work from only two defensive sets instead of the standard dozen or more. In Leach's early years at Tech, however, the defense often gave up as many or more points as the offense was able to put on the board. In the 2007 game against Oklahoma State, the Red Raiders lost by a score of 49-45 with the defense surrendering over 600 yards. When asked by a reporter what had happened, Leach responded, "The entire first half we got hit in the mouth and acted like somebody took our lunch money and all we wanted to do was have a pouty expression on our faces until somebody daubed our little tears off and made us feel better."

In a post-game meeting Leach so demeaned the defense that defensive coordinator Lyle Setencich resigned the next day. While Setencich said he was leaving for "personal reasons," there was speculation that Leach fired him. This must have been a difficult situation for Leach because Setencich was not just an assistant; the two had been friends all those years since Setencich had given Leach his first coaching job at Cal Poly-San Luis Obispo. Whatever the truth, Leach immediately moved his assistant head coach Ruffin McNeill, who had been with him at Tech since 2000, into the position. Under McNeill's leadership the defense steadily improved over the remainder of the season.

Tech fans—and football enthusiasts across the country—found Leach's high flying offense and improved defense exciting to watch. Opposing coaches did not always share their enthusiasm. For decades football centered on the running game known as "three yards and a cloud of dust." Legendary University of Texas Coach Darrell Royal was often quoted as saying that only three things could happen when a team passes the ball—two of those were bad (incomplete or interception). Most coaches and television analysts still emphatically claim that to be successful in passing, the team must first establish a running game. Only in the last couple of decades have a few coaches, notably Leach, depended on the pass as the first—and often second, third, and final—option.

Leach's success at Tech drew fans across a wide spectrum. Business magnate Donald Trump introduced the Red Raider offense and defense in their nationally televised game on ESPN against Oklahoma University on November 17, 2007. Trump declared that Leach "is my friend and one of the best coaches in the country." A year later, prior to the matchup with Oklahoma State on November 8, 2008, Trump appeared on ESPN's *College*

GameDay to again praise Leach calling him "an amazing guy."

The Leach offense is difficult for opposing coaches to prepare for not only because they risk being defeated by a system they do not endorse but also because they may suffer humiliating losses by large scoring margins. During Leach's tenure, Tech was often accused of running up the score. In his *New York Times* article Lewis explained, "His [Leach's] offensive machine lacked an off switch."

And the Leach offense plays full out until the last whistle blows. Leach does not use his second or third team to run out the clock but pushes them to move down the field and score. If he has to call a time out with seconds left to get in another play—even if leading by several touchdowns—Leach calls it.

Leach explains his "keep scoring" philosophy, "The interesting thing about football is that football is the only sport where you quit playing when you get a lead. In golf, you keep trying to score well when you're ahead. In basketball, they don't quit shooting when they're ahead. In hockey, they don't quit shooting when they're ahead. In boxing, you don't quit punching when you're ahead. But in football, somehow, magically, you're supposed to quit playing when you are ahead."

This style of football, of course, makes the traditional postgame handshake between coaches difficult. In an article by Bruce Feldman on ESPN.com on April 25, 2005, Leach explained, "Its uncomfortable. If I've lost, I don't feel like shaking your hand, and if I've won, you're probably not feeling like shaking mine."

Off the field, however, Leach gets along quite well with his fellow coaches. Former assistants speak well of him and he is close friends with many of his rivals. Today he is a frequent speaker on campuses across the country and he has no problem getting coaches to appear on his radio program.

Among Leach's achievements, the most striking is his ability to be a consistent winner using players who are not otherwise highly recruited. Superstar high school football players in Texas sign with the University of Texas or Oklahoma, a few with Texas A&M. Still others go to Nebraska, Michigan, Notre Dame, or to the major schools in Florida and California. Each year nearly every Top 25 team boasts at least one standout athlete from Texas. Texas Tech gets whatever is left over.

Dave Cisar, writing in wordpress.com on April 16, 2011, explains, "He was always going to have to settle for the second and third tier players. He focused on bringing in fast, smart kids that were maybe a bit undersized or odd shaped, kids that maybe didn't look like football players."

Four examples of Leach's recruiting acumen are Michael Crabtree, Matt Williams, Wes Welker, and Danny Amendola. Crabtree played quarterback at David W. Carter High School in Dallas and experienced more recruiting action than the usual Tech player. The University of Texas courted him, though with the caveat that they would convert him into a defensive back. Texas A&M, Baylor, Kansas, Kansas State, Oklahoma, Iowa, and Illinois all wanted to sign him either as a quarterback or as an "athlete" with a position to be determined.

Leach won the recruiting wars and signed Crabtree as a quarterback. According to a June 2011 interview with Crabtree, "On my first day of practice Leach noted my abilities to catch the football and I began to work as a wide receiver." For Crabtree, who later summarized that he "wanted to score touchdowns," it was an excellent decision. He was named to the All-American team in 2007 and 2008 as a receiver and in 2008 finished fifth in the Heisman Trophy competition. He then declared for the NFL draft where he was selected tenth in the first round by the San Francisco 49ers.

No one anywhere recruited Matt Williams. He enrolled in Tech as a regular student and then heard about a half-time competition being held during the Tech-University of Massachusetts game at Jones Stadium on September 20, 2008. Having honed his skills as a high school place kicker in Weatherford, Texas, Williams entered the contest in hopes of winning the sponsor's "free rent" prize for anyone who could kick a 30-yard field goal. Williams split the goal posts.

Leach, unhappy with his present kicker, admired Williams's

fundamentals and his ability to perform under pressure. A month later, Williams went from student to starter and made his debut against Kansas going 9 for 9 on points after touchdowns (PATs) earning him the honor of AT&T Player of the Week. By the end of the season he had successfully kicked 29 of 29 PAT attempts.

Wes Welker is much more typical of Leach's recruits. At five-foot-nine and weighing only 185 pounds, Welker was considered too small to play college football when he graduated from Heritage Hall High School in Oklahoma City. No one offered him a scholarship in Division I except Mike Leach. In four years at Tech he set punt return records, scored 21 touchdowns, and, in 2003, won the Mosi Tatupu Award for the best special teams player in college football. In 2004 Welker joined the National Football League. Welker, currently playing for the New England Patriots, is a three-time All-Pro and has been selected for the Pro-Bowl on three occasions.

Danny Amendola is also a typical Leach's recruit. Standing 5 feet 11 inches tall and weighing 183 pounds, Amendola did not attract the attention of many major colleges when he came out of The Woodlands High School north of Houston as a receiver in 2005. Leach saw that Amendola would fit into his formula as a wide receiver and punt returner. Amendola recalled in an April 2011 interview that he signed with Leach "because of Mike and his style of offense."

Amendola says, "I embraced his style of putting points on the board. The city of Lubbock embraced Mike. He had a great ability to relate to the student body. Everyone loved his aggressive style, going for it on 4th down no matter where you where on the field. He knew how to get a crowd into the game.

"It was not always easy," Amendola admits. "I did not enjoy rolling in sand pits for 20 minutes before practice or the up and downs and other exercises when we did not execute properly. But we knew that on Saturday we were going to score a lot of points, have fun, have a blast."

Amendola went undrafted by the NFL but then signed as a free agent with the Dallas Cowboys in 2008 before being cut and joining the Philadelphia Eagles. Again waived, he signed with the St. Louis Rams where he found a home as a receiver and punt returner. He led the NFL in all-purpose yards with 2,364 in the 2010 season.

Before he joined the NFL, Amendola accomplished something else at Texas Tech: he received his bachelor's degree. While that might appear to be an obvious outcome for a college student and athlete, the fact is that fewer than half of the college football players in the country actually complete their studies and graduate with diplomas. Of all Leach's accomplishments, perhaps the greatest—yet least heralded—is his success in demanding that his athletes be students. Leach and his assistants monitor the players' class attendance and their grades. When one of his Tech players missed classes and had poor scores, Leach sat him at a desk in the middle of the practice field where he studied rather than participated with the team in drills.

In 2008 Leach's players had a graduation rate of 79%, the highest in the Big 12. Only 46% of the University of Oklahoma players earned their diplomas while the University of Texas football players achieved a 50% rate. When Tech, Oklahoma, and Texas ended up in a three-way tie for the championship of the Big 12 South in 2008, Leach suggested that the tie-breaker be the player graduation rate. He found no takers.

Chapter 5

Leach and Tech Administrators: Early Conflicts

The first nine years of the Leach era at Texas Tech showed a steady improvement in the university's football program, the teams' posting winning records despite playing in the highly competitive Big 12 Conference. Tech quarterbacks, mostly ignored by other major program recruiters, led Division I passing eight of those nine years. For five of the same nine years, Tech led the country in total offense. Stadium seats filled, fans cheered, and national attention focused on the pass-happy team from the Texas plains. Players and their parents celebrated, too, as the graduation rate of Tech football players ranked at the top of the conference and nation.

Leach was happy with the Tech administration and they with him—at least in the early years. He got along well with John Montford, who was the Tech Chancellor from 1996 to 2001, and with David Smith, who filled that position from 2001 to 2006. Leach and Smith still maintain their friendship, talking frequently on the telephone. It was not until the arrival of Kent Hance in 2006 that Leach had any problems with the chancellor's office.

Although Tech President Guy Bailey played an important role in Leach's eventual dismissal, the two generally got along well, based partially on what appeared to be an equal dislike and mistrust of Chancellor Hance. Leach also had a good relationship with previous university presidents, David J. Schmidly 2000-2002 and Jon S. Whitmore 2002-2008.

While Mike Leach had not been what West Texas or Lubbock expected, winning teams had a way of ameliorating those first impressions—at least on the surface and certainly for the fans. Leach remained mostly oblivious to petty complaints and gossip. He concentrated on his teams, gaining the reputation as one of the conference's most accessible and open coaches. Leach always prioritized in favor of his teams, doing what he thought best for the program. Inevitably, though, with a traditional administration and a free-thinking coach, there was bound to be conflict.

From the beginning, tension over financial matters developed among the administrators, the athletic staff, and the football program. When highly acclaimed and equally controversial basketball coach Bobby Knight arrived at Tech in 2001, then University President Schmidly took a great interest in the new coach. At the same time Schmidly was not happy with Athletic Director Gerald Myers and cut his overall budget. Myers, not wanting to add to the president's ill will, passed the cuts to the football budget leaving Knight's basketball funds intact. This led to a series of conflicts.

When Myers reduced the football training meals' funds in April 2001, Leach was angered enough to send a memo of protest, noting, "Our football players need to be eating the same quality of meals as our opponents eat."

The struggle over money and control of it stretched taunt beneath the surface for months before it erupted in public awareness. The first incident, though minor, was a portent of things to come.

In May 2002 the university's vice president for fiscal affairs, Lynda Gilbert, stopped funding for the football program's outgoing postage because expenses for mail were $5,000 over-budget. In a series of memos between Leach and Gilbert over the next month, the coach noted, "We are not allowed to call recruits at this time [because of NCAA recruiting regulations] so mail service is vital. How do we regain equal footing with other programs in recruiting when they can send mail and we can't?"

Gilbert responded, according to articles later published by Brent Schrotenboer in the *Lubbock Avalanche-Journal*, with a dismissive reply, "The football program has not managed its funds well."

On June 29, 2002, Schrotenboer continued the story in the newspaper with quotes from Myers, who likely was still trying to keep Schmidly happy. Myers claimed that in addition to the over-budget postal category, the football program was actually $400,000 over-budget. He added that Tech was not Oklahoma, Texas, or A&M and, "...this is what we have at Texas Tech. We're going to do the best we can with what we have. I'm tired of hearing about what they do there. Maybe they [Leach and his staff] should get a job there if they think that's so great."

In what seemed like anger, Myers concluded, "We've given them [Leach's program] more than [former coach] Spike Dykes ever had."

The next day Schrotenboer reported that Leach, who was out of town on vacation, had retained local attorney Ted Liggett "to monitor the recent controversy surrounding the football program." The article quoted Liggett as saying Leach would hold a press conference upon his return to Lubbock. Quelling rumors that had begun about Leach's submitting his resignation, Liggett reassured the public, "Coach Leach has one thing on his mind, and that's to win football games."

In the same article President Schmidly initially fanned the controversy by stating, "I had hoped we could all get together and talk about it and take the high road and move on for the good of the program, but maybe that won't happen. It will be a real sad thing if it gets escalated before people can talk."

Schrotenboer quoted Schmidly as adding that he was "not mad" at Leach and that no disciplinary action had been discussed. He concluded, "I have no problem with Mike Leach. He's a damn good coach."

On July 9, Leach, Myers, and Schmidly sat down in what Schrotenboer reported was "an all-day meeting." The next day Leach and Myers held a press conference and read prepared statements. Myers stated, "We had a highly productive meeting on Tuesday and were able to discuss issues affecting the football program. Unfortunately, over the last few weeks, our schedules prevented us from meeting face to face to address these issues promptly and internally. In the heat of the moment, public comments were made that we all regret."

According to Myers, the budgetary issues had been the results of the football staff's spending $400,000 of the $1.62 million Tech expected to receive for an additional pre-Conference game—money that was not listed as anticipated income or in the original budget. Myers and Tech spokesperson Cindy Rugeley both assured the press that, in the future, budget matters would no longer be topics discussed in the media.

Leach called the entire matter a mere "blip on the radar screen." He added, "I think the administration, as well as the coaching staff, is passionate about what they do. Any time you have that energy and enthusiasm, it will carry you a certain distance. With people scattered around the country and things of that nature this time of year, I think our meeting was a great chance to get together and get headed the same direction."

This internal budget issue received little attention outside the university. Schrotenboer covered the controversy in as much depth as he did because he had used an Open Records Act Request to obtain the memos. Certainly outside of Lubbock there was little or no interest in the internal budget battle. It is noteworthy, however, that Leach's hiring of Liggett to represent his interests during periods he was out of town may have been a bell-weather of future actions. There were no official complaints or comments about their football coach retaining his own lawyer outside the university system, but surely Liggett's presence was not totally welcomed by Tech officials.

The monetary controversy disappeared for a couple of months, but strife over financial matters rose again, this time in a different form. On September 20, 2002, Schrotenboer reported in the *Avalanche-Journal*, "A sponsorship agreement worth $130,000 annually for Mike Leach's football camps and clinics has come apart in controversy after a heated eight-month dispute over money rights between Leach and Texas Tech administrators."

According to Schrotenboer, the dispute centered on who should receive grant money offered by ASCO, a Lubbock construction equipment company. The sponsor desired the funds be used strictly for the football camps and clinics but Athletic Director Myers and other Tech officials supposedly wanted the money for go into the university's general fund.

Leach, who would not personally receive any of the revenue, proposed that $90,000 go to camp scholarships for underprivileged youth to cover the salaries for camp staff and operational expenses. The other $40,000 would be retained by the university.

Myers backed down from wanting all the money to proposing that the university receive $100,000 with $30,000 dedicated to the camp. He further suggested that the school's amount could be used to pay for football player training-table meals that the budget shortfall deleted earlier in the year.

According to documents secured by Schrotenboer, the two sides continued the debate over the summer, arguing over just what Leach's contract called for in the directing of such funds. Finally, Bill Wright, the chairman of ASCO, wrote to Leach's agent Rick Davis complaining about how Tech was handling the matter, "I want to emphasize this has been the most unsatisfactory process I have ever encountered in all my 50 years of business experience."

Wright declared that if his donation went to the university's general fund rather than directly to the camps, he would withdraw his offer. Again Myers backed down and Wright contributed $90,000 to the camps for each of the next six years.

Learning from the previous budget battle, both Myers and Leach avoided any comments to the *Avalanche-Journal*. Again, the story garnered little interest or coverage outside the Lubbock market as the monetary tug-of-war between Tech and Leach continued.

By the end of the 2002 regular season Leach's teams had a record of 23-16 and had appeared in three revenue-producing bowl games. His winning record, along with the exciting offense, filled the seats at Jones Stadium, adding more income to the university's coffers. Despite the gains, Leach was still operating under his original five-year contract that guaranteed him an income of only $567,500 annually—the lowest amount of any coach in the Big 12 where all but three were receiving a million dollars or more per year.

Tech officials recognized that they had a winning, money-making coach, but they were reluctant to re-negotiate his contract. Instead they cautiously offered an addendum to his current agreement. In December 2003, Leach, working through his new agent Gary O'Hagan of the International Management Group (IMG), signed a one-year addendum committing his services through the 2005 season at a guaranteed salary of $752,500 per year. Even with the raise Leach's salary was still third from the bottom of Big 12 head coach wages.

Negotiations for a new contract began after the signing of the addendum. On April 12, 2004, Leach and Tech agreed to a five-year contract totaling $5,675,000. Leach had finally joined the million-dollar-a-year coaches club. Although some Tech administrators seemed resentful, they remained positive in their public statements. Myers was quoted in an *Avalanche-Journal* article by Don Williams on April 13, saying, "We've been working on it quite a while, and it's good to get it done and get it finalized, get an agreement in place that everybody feels good about."

In the same article Leach stated, "The biggest thing I'm satisfied with is that we got it squared away and that I can continue to zero in on coaching…."

For the next few years most of the news from Texas Tech and Mike Leach focused on the Red Raiders' style of football and their winning ways. The few controversies that did occur did not cause major news stories and had little negative impact on the team. Leach became known for running one of the cleanest, most rule-observant programs in college football.

While Leach was an honest, innovative, passionate coach and teacher at Tech, he was not perfect. He made mistakes; he learned from them. He did things his way. Some times so doing served him well; at other times it cost him dearly and unexpectedly. Mostly Leach did what he thought was best.

In October 2004, Texas Tech defeated Nebraska 70-10. Afterwards Leach heard his players arrogantly boasting to reporters that they would defeat Texas as well. From that time on, Leach restricted media access to his players. He personally remained extremely accessible and open about his activities and coaching style. This, of course, got him into trouble.

In his post-game press conference after the Texas game in 2007, Leach criticized the officiating crew for what he thought were bad calls. Leach suggested two possible causes: Either the officials were incompetent or, with the head official living in Austin, they wanted Texas to win and appear in a Bowl Championship Series (BCS) Bowl.

The Big 12 bosses were not amused, and they fined Leach $10,000—the largest assessment in conference history. Tech fans immediately set up a fund drive to pay the fine, but Leach requested the collected money go to buy 400 Christmas hams for needy Lubbock families. On New Year's Day Tech was again the victim of several bad calls in the Gator Bowl against the University of Virginia. When asked about the calls, Leach replied, "I don't comment on officiating. I just give out hams is what I do."

Leach did not allow the press to attend or film his talks with his team in the locker rooms. He did, however, permit the official Tech video crew to do so under the condition that only selected cuts would be made available for highlight reels produced for Red Raider booster clubs. These videos were considered to be for "in house use only" and were never to be released to the general public.

No one who has been around football practices and games is surprised to learn that many—if not most coaches—employ profanity to make their points. Leach was not an exception to the rule; he just ended up on YouTube.

Leach's public, on-the-record comments, also often created

controversy. One of his more famous comments came after an upset loss to Texas A&M on October 24, 2009. In a post-game interview he blamed the defeat on the team's complacency and the over-confidence inflated by praise from their "fat little girlfriends." The interview soon went viral on the internet, garnering laughs as well as complaints. Leach did not apologize but rather looked to the next game. Sales of the *Fat Little Girlfriends Cookbook* later became a fund raiser by Team Leach for a scholarship named in honor of the coach and presented to a Tech student.

These few incidents over nearly a decade were remarkably small in number and minor in infraction, especially compared to the charges of illegal recruiting practices, compensation of players, or personal misconduct—including DWIs and other crimes and misdemeanors—attributed to coaches at other major programs.

As Leach boosted his number of wins and earned a bowl game each season, his popularity among the fans rose and so did the revenues he brought in. During Leach's ten years at Tech, the university was able to invest more than $84 million dollars to enlarge and improve the team's stadium. Known as Jones Stadium and seating 53,000 when Leach arrived, the facility attracted a $1 million naming rights donation to become James AT&T Stadium in 2006. Tech's own revenues bought "the house that Mike built," as it is sometimes known, to a seating capacity of 60,454, a 175,000-square-foot press box with decks for television cameras, and luxury boxes and boxes for fans.

Chapter 6

The Golden Season: 2008

During its 2008 football season, Texas Tech achieved the best record in its history, set the attendance record for its Jones AT&T Stadium, won its biggest game ever, and climbed to its highest ever national ranking. For the first time ESPN's *College GameDay* did its pre-game telecast from the Tech campus. All eyes were on Lubbock, the Red Raiders, and Mike Leach. By the end of the season, Leach had risen from the ranks of "shining star" to "celebrity superstar." He was the topic of articles in major sports and general news publications, he made television appearances, and he visited with the President of the United States at the White House.

All the glory of the season was a far stretch from the unremarkable record the school had amassed since its initial outings. Texas Tech fielded its first football team in 1925 and for the next 83 years under 13 different coaches the teams managed to win only slightly more than half their regular season games and 12 of their 34 bowl contests. The Red Raiders did win eight Border Conference championships and one co-championship. After the university joined the Southwest Conference, its teams earned two co-championships. They had not won a division championship in the Big 12 and the Red Raiders had never finished in the Top 10 of the regular season National Polls.

No one ever seriously considered that Texas Tech would become a contender for the National Championship—that is, not until the spectacular season of 2008, which began the moment Tech concluded the 2007 season with a 31-28 final-second victory over the Virginia Cavaliers in the Gator Bowl. That 2007 team finished the season with a 9-4 record and a number 20 ranking in the polls. The Gator Bowl had barely concluded before national sportswriters began to talk about what a powerhouse Tech would be in 2008 and to speculate that the next season's team might compete for the National Championship.

Typical of the stories was an ESPN.com article by Mark Schlabach on May 7, 2008. Schlabach wrote, "Can't you imagine Leach standing on the field at Dolphin Stadium in Miami on the night of Jan. 8, holding a Waterford crystal trophy high above his head, smiling at the rest of the college football world with an eat-you-know-what grin?"

Schlabach then backed up his vision with speculation and data. He wrote, "Like the pirates who have fascinated the eccentric coach for much of his adult life, Texas Tech might be on the verge of robbing college football of its most cherished treasure this coming season. As long as Leach has resided in this close-to-nowhere town in west Texas, the Red Raiders have been equipped to launch an all-out assault. After he became their coach in 2000, they led the NCAA Division I-A in passing for five straight seasons and then again in 2007. Under his watch, Texas Tech has broken more than 150 NCAA, Big 12 and school records and scored 50 or more points in 21 games.

"And the Red Raiders might be more explosive than ever before during the 2008 season. Quarterback Graham Harrell, who last season led the country in total offense and became only the sixth player in NCAA history to throw for more than 5,000 yards in a season, is back for his senior year. Michael Crabtree, who set NCAA freshman records for receptions, receiving yards, and touchdowns last season, returns after winning the Fred Biletnikoff Award as the sport's top receiver. Eight other offensive starters are back, including all five lineman.

"But what is expected to make the 2008 Texas Tech team different from others in the past is its defense. Eight starters are expected to return to a unit that led the Big 12 in defense over the final eight games of the 2007 season."

Not every sportswriter was as high on Tech as Schlabach, but the Red Raiders received attention and respect across the country. Both *Sports Illustrated* and the Fox Sports Network rated Texas Tech number 10 in their pre-season poll. The Associated Press pre-season poll had them at number 12 while *USA Today* ranked them at number 14. Leach, Harrell, and Crabtree appeared on the cover of the 2008 edition of *Dave Campbell's Texas Football*. The magazine predicted that Tech would be the best college team in the state and would challenge Oklahoma for the Big 12 South title.

Games and championships are, of course, won on the field and not in the sports pages. Leach and his team were confident— not from their news coverage but because of their personnel and team preparation. In the first four weeks of the season, the Red Raiders defeated their non-conference opponents with easy victories over Eastern Washington 49-24, Nevada 35-19, SMU 43-7, and Massachusetts 56-14. Their national ranking rose from 14th to 8th.

Two weeks later the Red Raiders rolled over Kansas State by a score of 58-28 in their first conference matchup. While most universities generally schedule weak opponents for their homecoming game, Tech took on perennial power Nebraska for theirs. At the end of regulation the score for each totaled 31 points. Tech scored first in overtime but missed the extra point, to take a 37-31 lead. On the Cornhuskers' first play when they got the ball in overtime, Red Raider cornerback Jamar Wall intercepted a Nebraska pass, preserving the Tech victory and moving them up to 7th in the national polls.

An interesting sidelight from the game was the dispelling of the myth regarding "clock control." Contrary to the dictates of the general philosophy of football, the explosively victorious Tech offense had controlled the ball for only 19 minutes and 48 seconds during the game while the losing Cornhuskers possessed the ball for 40 minutes and 12 seconds.

Over the next two weeks the Red Raiders easily defeated Texas A&M 43-25 and Kansas 63-21. By now they had climbed to a number 5 ranking in the polls. On November 1 the University of Texas, rated number 1 in the nation, took the field at Jones Stadium before a record-breaking crowd. ESPN's *College GameDay* broadcast nationally from the Tech campus beginning hours before the kickoff. The stage had been set. The Tech-Texas game was the premier contest of the day—and the outcome proved to be the most outstanding victory in Red Raider history as well as one of the all-time greatest football contests in college sports.

Tech got on the board first, not with their offense, but with a two-point safety that resulted from the defense tackling a Longhorn running back in the end zone during the early minutes of the contest. The Red Raiders continued to dominate the first quarter, scoring a touchdown and a field goal while holding the Horns scoreless. In the second quarter Tech added another touchdown and field goal while giving up only two field goals. Tech led at halftime 22-6—and Leach's kicker Matt Williams, recruited from that early season half-time contest, accounted for eight of those points, two more than the entire Texas offense.

However, in the third quarter, Texas began to show why they were ranked number 1. Jordan Shipley ran a Tech punt back for a touchdown after Tech's Daniel Charbonnet intercepted a Colt McCoy pass for a touchdown. McCoy countered with a touchdown pass of his own but the two point conversion failed. At the end of three quarters, Tech led 29-19.

Early in the fourth quarter Tech made a sustained drive but had to settle for a field goal attempt that Texas blocked. On the next Longhorn play, McCoy threw a 91-yard touchdown that narrowed the Tech lead to 29-26 with 11 minutes remaining in the game. Tech controlled the ball for the next five minutes to net only another field goal. After the ensuing kickoff, the Longhorns marched 80 yards down the field to cross Tech's goal line once again. With the extra point they took their first lead of the game at 33-32 with only 1:29 remaining on the clock.

The Red Raiders returned the kickoff to their own 38-yard line where Harrell went to work. Four completed passes placed Tech on the Texas 28 yard line, but time was running out. Only 15 seconds remained. Harrell threw again. Almost intercepted, the pass dropped incomplete. With eight seconds left Harrell passed to Crabtree on the sideline at the six-yard marker. Crabtree caught the ball, broke a tackle, and crossed into the end zone with one second left on the clock.

Tech players celebrated and fans mobbed the field. But there was one second left. Assessed two excessive celebration penalties, the Red Raiders finally kicked off from their own seven yard line. Tech then recovered a fumbled backward pass by the Longhorns to end the game. Final score: Tech 39, Texas 33. In a match up ranked as the fifth most watched regular season game in television history, Texas Tech had beaten number 1; Tech had solidified its role as a national power by rising to number 3; and Mike Leach became one of the most talked about football coaches in America. For the first time two words circulated around the Tech campus: National Championship.

Leach and the Red Raiders, however, had little time to celebrate. The next week they faced the number 9 team in the country. Oklahoma State had beaten Tech the previous year during the Cowboys' last possession. That defeat had resulted in Leach's appointing a new defensive coordinator—a turning point, according to many of the Red Raider players.

The golden season of 2008 continued. At half time Tech led Oklahoma State 28-14. When the final gun sounded Tech ruled by 56-20. In the following national polls Tech moved into the number 2 spot, the highest ranking ever for a Texas Tech football team.

Week 10 of the 2008 season pitted the 10-0, number 2 ranked Red Raiders against 9-1, number 5 ranked Oklahoma in a nationally televised game on November 22. Despite their lower ranking, the Sooners went into the game a seven point favorite primarily because of their home field advantage. Sportswriters speculated that the winner of the game would play for the BCS Championship and that the victor's quarterback, either Tech's Harrell or OU's Sam Bradford, would win the Heisman Trophy. What followed was one of the greatest collapses in Tech football history. Oklahoma led from the beginning and won easily.

Plagued by penalties and a strong Sooner defense, the Red

Raiders could not muster much offense in the first quarter. Quarterback Harrell, who had been caught behind the line of scrimmage only five times the entire season, was sacked twice. At the end of the quarter OU led 7-0. In the second quarter Tech failed on a fourth down attempt, had a Harrell pass intercepted, and managed to score only a single touchdown. Oklahoma took advantage of every Tech misstep and added five touchdowns to lead 42-7 at half time.

Down by 35 points, the Red Raiders unsuccessfully attempted an on-side kick to open the second half. Then on their second possession Tech fumbled. They did not score until the final minutes of the quarter. Meanwhile, OU added 16 more points to their total to lead 58-14 at the end of the third.

In the fourth quarter Tech again failed to convert on fourth down, which led the Sooners to another touchdown. Tech finally scored their third touchdown with 11 seconds remaining in the game. In a "never say it's over until it's over spirit," Tech recovered the ensuing onside kick, but time had run out on Tech's victory chances long, long before. Final score: Oklahoma 65, Tech 21. The Red Raiders dropped to number 8 in the national polls.

Leach made no excuses for the loss except to say that it is difficult to defeat four top 20 teams in a row. When asked whether Texas or OU should rank higher in the next poll, he responded that his Coach's Poll vote would go to OU because "they beat us and they deserve it."

Some analysts noted that Tech had had a two-week break before the game and apparently came out rusty and unprepared. A few observed that Tech's game plan differed little from that of the year before. Others said that OU coach Bob Stoops knew how to defend against the Tech offense because Leach had spent a year as his assistant. Still others concluded that any team can have a bad day, including Tech. Many simply said the best team won. Whatever the cause, the Red Raiders had experienced the worst of the worst.

The size of the loss and the loss itself were significant, but Tech remained one of the few 10-1 teams in the country and the season was not yet over. A win over Baylor would still guarantee at least a part of the Big 12 South championship as well as a shot at a BCS bowl game. However, the OU game had been brutal in more than the final score. Two of the Tech defensive secondary starters were out with injuries.

After the opening kickoff with Baylor, Tech scored on their first possession only to give up two touchdowns to the Bears before the end of the quarter. Michael Crabtree injured his right ankle in the second and did not return for the rest of the game. The two teams traded scores and went into halftime with Baylor leading 21-14.

Baylor opened the third quarter with another touchdown, but it would be their last. Tech scored once before the end of the third and then added two touchdowns in the final quarter while holding Baylor scoreless for the remainder of the game to win 35-28.

Graham Harrell, who would ultimately lose the Heisman to Sam Bradford in the post-season announcement, showed his tenacity and competiveness against Baylor. In the second quarter he shattered two fingers on his non-throwing hand. At half-time medical staff x-rayed the hand and told Harrell he was through for the day. He responded, "Tape my hand up. I'm going out." It later took four hours of surgery, 17 pins, and two plates to repair Harrell's hand.

The victory over Baylor earned Tech a tie with Texas and OU, each with one loss, for the Big 12 South Championship. The tie breaker came down to BCS poll rankings, which meant Tech was not only out of the Big 12 Championship game but also eliminated from a BCS bowl game competition as well. Not all was bad, however: Tech got invited to the Cotton Bowl; Leach and Harrell were invited to the White House.

Two weeks after the Baylor game, Coach Mike Leach and his quarterback got a private tour of the President's White House home and then met for 20 minutes with George W. Bush. According to an article by Don Williams on redraiders.com on December 13, 2008, when Leach introduced himself to the president, Bush replied, "I know who you are. You don't have to introduce yourself." When Graham Harrell also started to introduce himself, Bush said, "I know who you are, too."

The Cotton Bowl call against Ole Miss did not go as well as the one to the White House. Tech went into the game a four-and-half-point favorite and outscored the Rebels 14-7 in the first quarter. Ole Miss went ahead in the second quarter, outscoring Tech 17-7 for a 24-21 half time lead.

Ole Miss scored on an interception early in the second half and led 38-21 at the end of the third quarter. Tech outscored the Rebels 13-9 in the fourth but when the game ended Tech had lost—the highest scoring game in Cotton Bowl history—47-34.

The loss was a disappointment to Leach and Tech fans, but they were proud of their 11-2 record that included victories over three ranked opponents and a share of the Big 12 South Championship.

The Maxwell Football Club, bestower of the highest and most prestigious coaching award, honored Mike Leach as its Coach of the Year for 2008.

It had truly been a golden season—the best in the history of Texas Tech football.

Chapter 7

The Turning Point:
New Contract Negotiations

The value of football coaches is calculated in a very simple manner. The coaches who win are worth more. And winning coaches themselves get recruited by other schools that promise more money and benefits. When Tech completed the 2008 season with an 11-2 record, Mike Leach was a highly valued commodity at the height of his marketability. Schools across the country— including Washington, Auburn, and Tennessee—expressed interest in the coach. If Tech wanted to keep him, they had to negotiate a new contract.

Negotiations between a victorious coach and a happy campus should have fairly easy. It was not to be. In 2007, before the Golden Season of 2008, President Guy Bailey expressed interests in renewing Leach's contract. Athletic Director Gerald Myers had difficulty coming to any decisions so Bailey reached out to Leach's representatives and came to a general agreement. Before terms for the new contract could be agreed upon, however, Tech regents and big-donor boosters—legally barred from the talks— apparently hijacked the negotiations.

These interlopers who were expressly prohibited from contract discussions by the Southern Association of Colleges and Schools (SACS) exchanged letters and emails among themselves indicating that they did not care if Leach left or stayed. In fact the chancellor, several regents, and some influential boosters went so far as to express their mutual interest in firing Leach as soon as possible—before or after the contract was signed. Contract talks resumed in the spring of 2008 but they remained contentious.

Several of these individuals had taken a strong personal dislike to Leach even before the negotiations. Curtis Parrish, a Lubbock lawyer and the public address announcer for Tech games at Jones

Stadium, summed up this animosity in a May 2011 interview. Parrish, who says he has no side in the debate—though he does favor his employer Texas Tech—said, "Mike Leach did not glad-hand the big donors and influential alumni, he is not a salesman, he does not speak all that well, and is often profane and vulgar; all he wants is to be left alone to coach football. He rubbed some people the wrong way and just did not fit in with what is considered Lubbock standards."

In fact Leach raised more resources than any football coach in Tech history. He routinely accepted invitations to speak to fans, boosters, and donors. The resources his teams generated not only remodeled Jones Stadium three times; he filled ever seat built.

It is also noteworthy that the Tech administrators did not view Leach as "their guy." He had been hired under a previous university president, chancellor, and board. New administration officials—and certainly some of the regents—were looking for a coach who would be in lockstep with them, not an independent freewheeler. Interacting more from impressions than first-hand acquaintance, the coach and the administrators did not know each other well. Their first major interaction would be to negotiate a multi-million dollar contract.

What began as dislike for an outsider with a different temperament soon ratcheted up to what appears to be nothing short of loathing. Certainly some of the powerbrokers on the Board of Regents as well as influential donors accustomed to calling the shots were offended when a mere football coach, represented by his "city slicker Yankee agents," bested them in the talks and on the contract deal. Several of these individuals, "men of substance" as described in their own Board of Regents Rules, seemingly began to plot to punish Leach. According to their emails among themselves, they hoped that he would not sign the new contract; if he did, they would look to find reasons to fire him before he would be due any financial bonuses.

Coaches' contracts mean more than just money and benefits. University coaches with long-term contracts are more attractive to recruits who are wary of signing with a program where the head coach might be gone before they participate in their first practice. It is very likely Tech would have gotten off cheaper in the contract negotations and built an even stronger team if the university had been willing to renegotiate Leach's contract in the spring of 2008 before the Golden Season of that fall. But they were not.

In fact, on April 16, 2008, Leach's agents at IMG wrote to Tech's Deputy Athletic Director Bobby Gleason with a proposal for a contract extension of $15.25 million over five years. Nine days later Matt Baldwin, also with IMG, sent another letter to Gleason and Athletic Director Myers, stating, "I received a call from Bobby Gleason this afternoon, during which he informed me that it is the intention of Texas Tech University to table all discussions on a contract extension for Mike Leach until the conclusion of the 2008 football season...I must say that this response came as both a major surprise and disappointment. The decision to let Mike's contract run down to having two years remaining on the term will have disastrous consequences to the Red Raider football program in many areas, including coach contentment, negative recruiting and poor public relations."

On April 29, AD Myers took the position that not only was Tech not in a financial position to pay such lucrative salaries but he also appeared to insinuate that he really did not care if Leach remained in Lubbock or not. Myers stated, "We regret we are unable to consider your request for changes in Mike Leach's contract at this time. Mike has an excellent contract. Our financial conditions for the overall athletic program cannot afford such increases when we consider plans for the future.

"We realize Mike Leach's talents. He is an excellent coach. His desire to make more money is perfectly logical, but we have about reached the limits of what we can pay our coach and still maintain the rest of the department.

"If better opportunities occur for him somewhere else, we will fully understand."

Little communications on the subject, and none that produced any progress, occurred over the next half-year. Not until the Tech victory over Texas resulted in a 9-0 record and a number 2 national ranking did Tech's athletic director finally announce that the university would renegotiate Leach's contract at the end of the football season and offer him an extension.

On December 5, 2008, Myers made a contract extension proposal to Leach through IMG, including an offer of $12.1 million over five years. IMG then presented a counteroffer of $14.25 over five years on December 16, both actions in the fashion of typical offers and counteroffers in football-coach contract negotiations. But at this point in the procedure other factors and individuals entered into the talks, adding to the tensions and causing long-term impact on the coach-university relationship.

Texas Tech University Chancellor Kent Hance, Board of Regents members Larry Anders and Jerry Turner, and former board members Jim Sowell and Alan White began a series of emails, phone conversations, and meetings in an effort to influence the negotiations. These five men appeared to share a devotion to Texas Tech, each seemed empowered by a large personal fortune, and all appeared to dislike Mike Leach—feelings that would intensify as the negotiations progressed.

Kent Hance, the chancellor—the executive having the responsibility for the entire Texas Tech System—had himself graduated from Tech in 1965. He was admitted to the bar upon his graduation from the University of Texas Law School in 1968. After practicing law in Lubbock for five years, he entered politics, winning a seat in the Texas Senate where he served until 1979. He then ran against George W. Bush to represent the 19th Congressional District. In his campaign Hance repeatedly emphasized Bush's privileged upbringing and his Yale education, claiming he was not "a real Texan."

Hance, often referred to as "the Reverend," also emphasized Bush's alleged drinking problems—although the future chancellor had been part owner of a Lubbock bar named Fat Dawg's for years before selling it prior to his run for Congress. According to a *New York Times* article by Nicholas D. Kristof on July 27, 2000, Hance continued to own the building and collected lease money from the bar during and after the election.

The same article noted that when Bush offered free beer to Tech students rallying on his behalf, "A law partner of Mr. Hance wrote a public letter denouncing the Bush campaign for using alcohol to lure young people. The letter went to 4,000 members of the Church of Christ in Lubbock, and copies were put under windshield wipers of cars of people attending church services."

The strategy worked with Hance winning by seven percentage points, the only time the future 43rd President of the United States lost a general election.

As a Democrat, Hance won reelection to Congress twice before leaving to run for a Senate seat, which he lost in a close election. In 1985 he switched to the Republican party and ran unsuccessfully for Texas governor. He failed in another attempt to gain the governor's office in 1990. On December 1, 2006 he took a leave of absence from his Austin law firm to assume the chancellorship of the Texas Tech System.

Hance, known as a man who insists on being in charge and who enjoys the seat of power, also has a long record as a hardball negotiator. In 1995, Hance worked as a lobbyist for Waste Control Specialists, a company that disposes of a broad range of hazardous wastes, among them low-level and mixed radioactive products. An article in the May 23, 1995, edition of the *Houston Chronicle,* later referenced in the March 27, 2001, edition of *Lobby Watch*, reported that in an effort to secure authorization for a dump site in Andrews County in far West Texas, Hance and fellow lobbyists John Birdwell were accused of trying to bribe Representative Robert Talton with a job and $60,000 in donations for his support. Both lobbyists denied the accusations and no legal action resulted. The same edition of *Lobby Watch* also stated that Hance contributed $151,023 to various political candidates from 1997 to 2000.

In 2003, Waste Control Systems finally received authorization for a nuclear waste dump, and the company has since lobbied to increase its capacity and to import waste from throughout the United States. Andrews County locals and national environmentalists continue their opposition, claiming that the dump is polluting the Ogallala Aquifer, the largest water source in the central United States.

Hance remains associated with Waste Control Systems today. He is a part owner and the vice chairman of its Board of Directors.

The chancellor also appeared to have engaged in other questionable business practices. An article in the July 5, 2007 edition of *Texans for Public Justice*, titled "Watch Your Assets: Exposing the misuse and abuse of the public commons," covered the history of corruption and abuses in the awarding of federal tax breaks to private companies for building affordable housing. The article stated, "Landmark Affordable Housing, run by lobbyist and ex-Congressman Kent Hance and his children, has received more than $36 million in tax credits for four TDHCA [Texas Department of Housing and Community Affairs] projects.... . Hance has contributed almost $335,000 to Texas political committees and candidates since 2004. Over the past decade he also has lobbied Texas officials on behalf of three low-income interests: Kilday Realty, Lankford Interests and the American Housing Foundation. TDHCA tax-credit recipient Edgewater Affordable Housing also hired Hance to lobby federal officials in 2005."

When Hance—a lean, balding, politically savvy man of polished manners—assumed the chancellorship and helm of the educational complex on the Plains, he did so with a definite plan in mind. Hance's driving goal has been to elevate Texas Tech to a nationally recognized tier-one institution of higher learning, an arduous undertaking that has involved restructuring departments, reprioritizing purposes, and expanding the system—and a lot of politicking in his previous haunts in the halls on Capitol Hill. Hance, a generous donor to both sides of the political aisle, makes an annual pilgrimage to Washington, D. C., to boast about Texas Tech's academic excellence and its wide-ranging research projects—many funded by those whose hands he is shaking.

To achieve his objectives, Hance evidently had no qualms about seeing the old guard personnel of the Texas Tech System replaced by individuals with whom he had a close relationship. High-ranking administrators and officials were quick to resign shortly after Hance arrived. Officially they left "to accept other appointments" or "for personal reasons," but everyone suspected what force was behind their new directions.

University President Jon Whitmore was one of the first to go, followed by many others. On June 25, 2008, James Clark of Lubbock's News Radio 1420, summed up the mass exodus when he announced that, in addition to Whitmore's resignation the previous year, more administrators were departing, including Walt Huffman as dean of the law school and Alexia Green as dean of the nursing school. Also gone were a half dozen other university vice presidents, numerous development officers, and two medical school administrators.

And then there was Mike Leach—an often crass pirate-lore-spouting coach standing immutable in the spotlight in the middle of Tech's most successful and nationally noted victories. Despite all of Hance's energy directed otherwise, football and athletics rather than the Chancellor were bringing Texas Tech to national attention.

Dave Walker, owner of several Lubbock radio stations that cover Tech and the university's sports programs, said in a June 2011 interview, "I know Mike Leach and Kent Hance both very well. Their showdown was inevitable. Both have strong personalities; neither will back down."

Conferring with and supporting Hance on the Board of Regents, for one, was Lubbock native and Tech graduate Larry Anders, the chairman and majority owner of Summit Alliance

Companies, a Dallas investment advisory and financial services firm. He joined the Board of Regents in 2005 and was reappointed in 2011, acting as vice chairman of the Board during Leach's contract negotiations. From March 2, 2009 to February 24, 2011 he served as chairman of the Board.

According to a 2010 report by the watchdog group *Texans for Public Justice*, Anders contributed $416,546 to Governor Rick Perry's campaign between 2001 and 2010. Perry is the governor who appointed Anders to the Tech Board of Regents.

Jerry Turner, also a Tech alumnus who graduated in 1968 after being the captain of the football team, was another regent and confidant of Hance's. He earned his law degree at Vanderbilt University before becoming a partner at Andrews Kurth, L.L.P. in Austin. Texas Governor Rick Perry appointed Turner to the Board of Regents in 2007, where he participated in the Leach contract negotiations as a board member. Turner became the Board's vice chairman before assuming the chairmanship in 2011.

Also among Hance's regular email correspondents on the subject of the future of Texas Tech were some devoted boosters who generously contribute to the university's coffers. One of them was yet another Tech graduate Jim Sowell. He formed Jim Sowell Construction Company in 1972, an organization which grew to become one of the largest subdivision developers in Texas. His business, now known as Sowell & Co., is based in Dallas. According to Larry Burton, featured columnist on bleacherreport.com, in an article on January 9, 2010, "Sowell made his money in construction and is used to getting in the dirt for results." Sowell is also a frequent contributor to political causes, giving $47,500 to then Governor George Bush in 2000, according to *Texans for Public Justice*.

Sowell served on the Tech Board of Regents from 1995 to 2001—prior to the Hance regime—so he was no longer playing a formal role in university business at the time of the Leach contract negotiations. Informally, however, he maintained contact with Hance, Anders, and Turner; he became what looked like the leading advocate in the movement to fire Leach, or at least to limit his contract.

Alan White, a 1972 Tech graduate who had previously served as chairman of the Board of Regents, also discussed continuing university concerns with Hance and some of the current board members. White, with his degree in finance, rose to become the Chairman of Dallas-based PlainsCapital Bank.

The resumes of these men include long lists of accomplishments as well as of the generous contributions they made to Tech and other organizations. Their philanthropic interests extend from community service and assistance to the Boy Scouts of America to religious organizations. By most accounts they are all honorable men with honorable intentions. However, like many of the rich and powerful, they appear at times to be more than willing to bend or, break a few rules in order to get what they want.

The participation of these men in the Leach contract negotiations is an excellent example of what many would call an abuse of position and power. According to the university's rules—Texas Tech University Policies and Procedures—and the guidelines issued by the SACS, the only persons authorized to negotiate a contact with the football coach were the university president and the athletic director—in this case President Bailey and AD Myers. In spite of these regulations, intended to prevent exactly what was about to happen, Hance—with the support and advice of regents Anders and Turner—directly entered into the talks with Leach. Furthermore, the three current board members began a dialogue with former members Sowell and White on how best to negotiate the contract.

This was not ignorance or naiveté on their parts. The later sworn depositions of Anders, Turner, and Bailey all demonstrated that they were aware of the Tech and SACS regulations and policies. In fact, Anders and Turner warned the others about what they were doing by circulating a news story about the probation imposed on Auburn University because of interference by its board of regents in its football program.

Neither Hance nor the regents—current or former—have ever overtly admitted that they did not want to extend Leach's contract—or that they believed that terminating his contract should be the course of action. They were only too well aware that not extending it after the Golden Season of 2008 would prove extremely unpopular and impossible to justify. With its 11-2 record, Texas Tech was in the grips of "pirate mania"—and surely the Tech officials retained the clear vision of students camping out overnight to get game tickets and the stands of Jones Stadium being full of fans wearing skull and crossbones shirts and other pirate regalia.

Still, completely ignoring the student delirium over a winning team, Leach's popularity among fans, and the financial impact of a full stadium, the chancellor, regents, and former regents continued their dialogue by telephone and email on the best courses of action to rid the school of Leach and the most effective ways to influence Athletic Director Myers and President Bailey in their negotiations. While there are no records of their phone conversations, several of the emails from Jim Sowell to Hance, preserved on the orders of the Chancellor to his secretary Linda Steele, were later revealed after an Open Records Request by the *Dallas Morning News*.

When these emails made their way to the public a year later, in December 2009, sports blogger Brooks Melchoir at sportsbybrooks.com noted on the 30th, "The emails may give some indication of an extremely acrimonious contract negotiation between Leach's reps at IMG last year and Tech administrators."

Melchoir continued, "Again, this email is from a prominent booster privy to the details of the 2008 Leach contract negotiations. If the email is any indication, it shows just how much animosity had built up between a Tech booster and possibly the school's administration and Leach. Considering Leach's stunning superficial success on and off-the-field, Sowell's vitriol-laced statements about the coach really are quite remarkable. Makes you wonder if Hance and Myers shared his view. Not unreasonable to think, in my opinion, that they did."

In the first referenced email between former board members, dated December 8, 2008, Sowell writes to White, with a copy going to Hance, that he thinks Leach is not all that marketable to other university programs, stating, "Leach doesn't have any other options, in my opinion, the only change we need to make is up his buyout penalty if he leaves and make sure if we fire him that we only owe him his remaining base salary of around $300,000 per year."

After the December 16 counter-proposal by IMG, Sowell emailed Hance, with a copy to Myers, on December 18, "Kent, their latest offer is offensive. Mike wants a salary virtually the same as Stoops and Brown, both of whom have national championships."

Sowell continued with a lengthy explanation about why he believed the IMG offer was out of line. He added, "I'm tired of the Mike Leach Contract Soap Opera."

In conclusion Sowell stated, "He has no bargaining power. If he just lives out the two years left on his contract and kills our recruiting, he will be committing professional suicide. What AD will want a guy who torched his previous program? Leach has been able to do one thing no Tech coach has ever been able to do before—make me disgusted with the Tech football program. You have made him an offer that is more than fair."

While Sowell's personal feelings are obvious in the email, his argument about "bargaining power" are not valid. Leach had completed nine extremely successful seasons culminating in a revenue-producing bowl game each year. Over that period his teams had amassed the third best record in the conference and Sowell wanted to offer a salary equal to the 10th best record—or worst might be a better description.

By December 30, Sowell remained against agreeing to IMG counter offers and, despite no longer having any official input, looked to the future when they could fire Leach. His email to Hance, with a copy to Myers, stated, "Kent, they have no leverage, don't give in. Also, I feel you should sign a contract that would not cost us too much to fire him."

In the days to come, Sowell would make lengthy comments on Leach's salary and his "Jerry McGuire wannabes" agents and conclude, "I promise you our prospects for getting a better coach are much higher than Mike's prospect of getting a better job.... Bottom line, we can't afford what he is asking for. Every $100,000 we give him is $1.5 million in improvements we could have bonded."

While Sowell appeared fixated on the salaries of others, he did not seem to question the compensation and perks the board approved for the chancellor. At the time he was negotiating Leach's contract, Chancellor Hance received generous stipends from the Texas Tech System. According to information secured by the *Lubbock County Register* in a 2009 Open Records Request, the chancellor's base pay was $412,000 per year plus a deferred salary of $229,500. Hance also received $2,000 per month in automobile expenses for a total annual compensation of $665,500. Travel expenses, sports tickets, and a Sky Box at Jones Stadium rounded out his entitlements. The *Register* summarized, "The contract is truly 'Lap of Luxury' funded by tax dollars."

Jerry Turner also detailed his opposition to the contract and his dislike of Leach. In a January 9, 2009 email to Hance and fellow board member Anders, Turner wrote, "Remember there are three fundamental characteristics of a pirate that people find most abhorrent—lack of loyalty to any country, lack of respect for others and incredible greed. Apparently not all pirates are in Somalia or along the Barbary Coast."

On January 9, 2009, AD Myers, as the appropriate Tech official to do the negotiating, emailed IMG a counteroffer that included $12.7 million over five years with a $600,000 bonus if Leach completed the contract. The new proposal also contained reduced salary benefits and new limiting provisions. These provisions dictated that Leach ask Tech for permission to interview with other universities for possible coaching positions during the period of the contract. If he did so without permission, he could be terminated with cause and fined $1.5 million. This proviso likely resulted from the anger that Hance and others felt when they learned that Leach had gone to Seattle after the Baylor game the previous December to talk with University of Washington officials.

Again, although the anger of Hance and his associates about Leach's looking at other coaching opportunities was real, they should have not been all that surprised that he would entertain interests from other schools. In AD Myers letter of April 29, 2008, and in the contract negotiations, Tech administrators had repeatedly told Leach that it might be best for him to look elsewhere for employment.

The second provision called for a reduction in the amount of money Leach would receive if he was fired without cause. His old contract called for 40% of his guaranteed money, the lowest in the Big 12; the new contract reduced that amount to less than 12%, the lowest in the nation among Division I coaches.

Provision number three increased the buyout clause— money to be paid to the university by Leach if he voluntarily left the program—from $500,000 to $1.5 million. The fourth provision declared that the university would assume all personal property rights (control of Leach's likeness in promotions and advertisements as well as possible book royalties) related to his coaching position, rights that Leach retained under the old contract.

In the end, egos and money won out over common sense and what would ultimately be good for Texas Tech. Myers, now acting on advice and influence from Hance, Anders, and Turner, concluded Tech's offer by saying that this was the university's "best and final offer." He set a deadline of January 20 for response.

Baldwin at IMG responded in less than seventeen minutes, not with another counter but with a chart of Big 12 coaches' current salaries, guaranteed amounts, and buyout clauses in their contracts. Myers obviously shared the response up the chain of command because Chancellor Hance forwarded it via email to former board member Sowell early that evening with a two-sentence message, "This is the response to our offer. We are going to ignore it."

Just before midnight Sowell emailed Hance back, "I hope he doesn't sign, that gives us a full year to find another coach after we fire him after next season and pay off the remaining year on his contract."

Sowell then discussed the announcement of the contract extension of Gary Patterson, head coach at TCU, saying "[Patterson] may have done the best job of any coach in the country the last 6 years. He probably makes half of what Leach does. Think of what we could do with that 1 million a year in savings."

Apparently Sowell had not done his homework. In 2008, Patterson earned $1.8 million—far more than Leach—and then TCU raised his salary to $2.5 million annually in 2009. By 2011, Patterson was earning $3 million with no buyout clause.

By placing a deadline of January 20 for Leach's decision, Myers had escalated the negotiations to a near breaking point. Sportsblog.com posted a guest contribution by Matthew J. Lopez, a Tech Law School student, on February 17 that explained the impact of the deadline. He wrote, "TTU's decision to maintain its stated reservation point (walk away point) and give Leach an ultimatum is considered a power technique in the world of negotiations. In this adversarial approach, a party treats the process as a zero sum game in which one side's gain is another side's loss, or put in other words, there must be a winner and a loser in the end."

More importantly, Chancellor Hance, his regent advisors, and big donors involved were gambling—via President Bailey and AD Myers—with a weak hand. Leach still had a contract for the next two years, and, as the negotiations dragged on, rallies on campus supporting Leach began. One fan even placed a full-page ad in the Lubbock newspaper blasting Tech officials for their failure to execute a new contract. Also, this was not "the first ball game" for the IMG agents—they represent more football coaches than any agency in the country and are the largest sports marketing and talent representation company in the world. They knew how to negotiate, and were not going to settle for less than what they considered the "fair market value" of their client.

Five days after the communiqué from AD Myers, on January 12, Baldwin from IMG formally replied, writing, "You made it clear that the included offer is final and that you are not open to further discussions or negotiations. Given that, I'm afraid we have no choice but to respectfully decline the offer." He continued by explaining that the monetary compensation was not the problem; rather, the four added provisions in the contract were a "significant step backward."

In essence Baldwin had called Myers' bluff on the deadline; however, he was still willing to negotiate—just at a new level. On January 15, Baldwin emailed most of the Board of Regents, thereby officially recognizing the involvement of the members and Tech's major donors, in the negotiation process. He did not, however, copy the message to AD Myers, President Bailey, or Chancellor Hance. Baldwin wrote, "We feel that there has been some misinformation about our position regarding the most recent contract offer made by Texas Tech. The feeling is based on some of the questions that Mike had been asked from some board members and boosters. In the interest of accuracy, we have prepared a chart which compares four elements of change that were introduced at the eleventh hour."

On January 16, an offended F. Scott Dueser, Board of Regents Chairman, responded in what appeared to be a huff, "I cannot adequately express the level of disappointment I feel that you would take the liberty of communicating directly with certain members of the Board of Regents regarding the status of your negotiations with Chancellor Hance, President Bailey, and Athletic Director Myers without at the very least showing them the courtesy and respect of receiving a copy of your communications. If your message was calculated to divide the Board or undermine the Chancellor, President, and Athletic Director, you have greatly misjudged us and the mutual respect we have for one another."

Dueser concluded by directing IMG to communicate only with the athletic director, president, and chancellor—even though the latter was clearly an inappropriate participant. IMG apologized, explaining that the three had been inadvertently left off the email list.

On January 20, Baldwin sent another email to AD Myers stating that Leach was willing to accept the $12.7 million over five years but was asking for an additional $1.15 million in incentive bonuses and as well as changes in the recently instituted limiting provisions.

Myers responded on January 26 with a summary of the negotiations over the past months and stated, "We want you as his agent to stop shopping Coach Leach everywhere and him not saying anything to deny that he's looking for another job.... Another issue that has come up is insubordination. It was wrong to go around Chancellor Hance, President Bailey, and myself to contact the Board of Regents individually."

In the message Myers made no mention of the previous January 20 deadline, now nearly a week in the past. He did say that he still wanted Leach to be Tech's coach and he set a new deadline of February 17 for an IMG response.

Baldwin answered in a January 28 email saying that, while the salary level was "acceptable," the conditions of the four new added provisions were not. He then answered Myers' accusation of insubordination, stating, "Just to be clear, to be insubordinate, you first need to be subordinate. IMG is retained by Coach, not by Texas Tech; and thus IMG cannot be insubordinate to Texas Tech."

In conclusion, Baldwin wrote, "We, like you, remain hopeful that Coach will remain the head football coach at Texas Tech for many years to come. However, absent a significant change in Texas Tech's position in this negotiation, it is highly unlikely that an agreement can be reached for the aforementioned reasons."

On February 6, 2009, Myers wrote that the Tech offer still stood but he did not say what would happen if an agreement were not reached by the February 17 deadline. He did add that the deadline "pretty well explains itself."

Gary O'Hagan of IMG volleyed back saying that he thought Leach would be at Tech for the next two years and would field "two great teams." In other words, he did not think a new contract would come to fruition.

Most sports writers and bloggers agreed. It appeared that an impasse had been reached and that Leach's tenure at Tech would be limited to the final two years of his current contract, or as some ventured, the university would fire him soon after the newest contract deadline passed.

Meanwhile pro-Leach rallies continued on campus. Leach spoke out on radio talk shows about the negotiations, gaining additional support for his contract stance. The Tech administration finally seemed to realize just how unpopular a decision to let Leach go would be.

There are few emails and no records of the telephone conversations that took place between the administrators, regents, and boosters over the next two weeks, but what is available is revealing. Even anti-Leach, big donor Jim Sowell was getting the message. In response to unreleased emails titled "Re: Leach Fiasco," Sowell wrote Chancellor Hance, Deputy Athletic Director Gleason, and AD Myers on February 7, "Also we need to make sure the public knows that permission for Leach to interview will not be unreasonably withheld and that notification of the interview will allow our AD to call the other AD to confirm the seriousness of the interest so that the 'interview' can't be used as a negotiating tactic, as it has been in the past."

Another one of the emails secured and made public by the *Dallas Morning News* summed up the contentiousness of the negotiations and provided the most reasonable solution to the contract debacle. The writer identifies himself as a long-time Tech booster and, based on the content of the email, he appeared to have a close relationship with Leach, Hance, and the others involved in the negotiations. His actual identity was redacted from the released copy of the mail sent to Hance with a simple subject line of "Mike."

The lengthy message begins, "Kent, I told Mike to call you tomorrow and get one on one with you. Regardless of what you think, he has feelings and is sensitive. Gerald [Myers] has always had a hard time with Leach which goes back to Schmidley and Smith. I am going to say a few things and get them off my chest as a long time fan and businessman. I do not expect you to like what I say, or respond in any fashion. I do not expect you to change your mind, but, I am writing this as an objective outsider who has watched TT for 48 years now."

The message continues, "As in most small schools TT has its small clique of large donors, Regents, its President or Chancellor or in our case both that talk in small groups and form their opinions and make decisions about everything for their school. You all have done a wonderful job of leading TT to the next level of National Prominence. Academically and sports with Knight and Leach have made Tech a household name in recent years. You will have to admit Knight and Leach are very odd and different people compared to your inner circle of West Texans and large donors to TT. I doubt very seriously if anyone but Bob Knight would have gotten away with what he did at Tech, including chasing the Chancellor down street, and, he wouldn't have gotten away with that if it hadn't been for Gerald's close relationship with him. On the other hand you have a situation where you have a football coach who with the strong support of TT, has filled the stadium, sold all the suites, been to 9 straight bowls, has the third best record in the conference since he's been here, etc....Most importantly, again with TT's strong support, but, on his watch they have recruited and have the highest graduation rates for white and minorities in the conference. Our two best recruiting years have been the last two, and every comment from the players talk about how they connect to the staff and Mike, like him or not he is performing magic....Mike is...is not a "good ol' boy," he's a quirky intellect who is a football coach. Love him or hate him, you guys should not be bowing your necks and running him off because you can't get along with or relate

63

to some city slicker Yankee agent. I agree that you need to make some changes to his contract, but, they should be done in a spirit of good will and privately. I am guessing his requirements are not any different than the other coaches contracts in the league, and, only 2 have been more successful than he has."

In the final paragraph the unnamed booster said, "I know all about the 'courting' of other schools, but, I know, you know, and Mike knows there are only 10 or 12 better jobs in the country, and, you would only say better because of recruiting possibilities because of tradition. With only 2 years left and shaky relationship with the AD, he shouldn't close too many doors, those are my words, not his, but, I know how he is feeling. You know all of the above, but, I want to tell you with all that in my mind you people would be crazy to end this great period of TT football on a negative note. Make a deal with him, reconcile publicly and if he craps on you later, then it's shame on him. In my mind, if we simply shut him out or fire him, it is shame on us. I told him and will tell you, ego and pride have brought many people down, so let's get off that inner circle ego trip and get this done. I watch the BB games with any [sic] empty arena and I get sick, don't do that to football as well. We are on top of the world as you say 'for our budget,' let's stay there."

Despite this email and pressure from other boosters, the February 17 deadline passed with no further action. The only activity on the deadline date was a rally by several dozen students and Lubbock residents outside Leach's office. The coach made a brief appearance to thank his supporters. One student carried a sign saying, "Keep Leach or walk the plank."

Tech officials did not comment on the deadline. Indeed, they ducked the issue. *USA Today* noted in an article on February 19, "A call to Chancellor Kent Hance was not immediately returned." The article continued, "Scott Dueser, the chairman of the school's Board of Regents, did not immediately respond to a voice mail message and an email seeking comment."

The only action by Tech was an announcement late on the afternoon of the 17th that the Board of Regents would hold a "special teleconference meeting" on the 20th to discuss Leach's contract and his future with the university. On the 18th Leach requested that the scheduled closed board meeting be made a public hearing. Under state provisions, his request was granted. The meeting, however, would not be necessary.

According to Don Williams, writing in the *Lubbock Avalanche Journal* on February 20, "Hance and Myers had long expressed a desire to negotiate with Leach face-to-face. Hance credited Ted Liggett, Leach's personal lawyer, with helping make it happen." What was missing from the story was the fact that it was Hance who caved to the pressure and contacted Liggett, seeking terms of what in essence was surrender.

Hance and Leach sat down early on the afternoon of February 19 for a 30-45 minute conversation—of which only 15 minutes or so were dedicated to the contract itself. Publically, Tech officials claimed the meeting lasted two-and-a-half hours. At the end of the meeting they agreed to extend Leach's remaining two-year contract for three more seasons for $12.7 million. The two sides agreed to take out the buyout clause altogether and to raise the guaranteed money from $1.5 million to $2 million. Leach would now be free to interview for other jobs of his choosing and would only have to notify Tech officials of his visits to other campuses, not get their permission or "hall pass" as it had become known. Leach retained his personal property rights.

Now it was time for both sides to make nice—at least publically. At the post-meeting news conference Hance stated, "We'll just make that zero on the buyout. I know he's not leaving."

AD Myers attended the news conference and added that he always wanted Leach to remain as coach. He said, "To put it mildly, this has been a tough negotiation. It's been a tough time, and it's really good to get it behind us. I know a lot of you [in the media] said we wouldn't get it done. I think everybody concerned is pleased with the agreement we have in place."

Leach responded, "Me and my family are thrilled to death that we're going to be in Lubbock for another five years. It's become a part of our family. At the rate I get folks saying 'We just don't know if you like Lubbock,' it's like I don't know how we can get rooted in here any deeper than we already are. So I've decided that rather than mess with that, I'm going to say I love Lubbock every single press conference. My family all loves Lubbock, and I appreciate Chancellor Hance and Gerald's efforts to allow us to stay here and the opportunity to coach for the Red Raiders for what I hope is many years to come."

Thus concluded the formal contract soap opera saga of Mike Leach and Texas Tech University. Finally, it appeared that the participants had reached the end of the beginning of the tensions between Tech administrators and Mike Leach. In reality, the contract closure was the beginning of the end for the coach's tenure at Texas Tech.

Leach made no further comment about the contract negotiations nor did he say anything about bad feelings against his bosses. If he harbored any ill will against them, and surely he must have, he put it aside. After all, he had come out of the negotiations with a lucrative, long-term agreement. Now he wanted to get back to coaching and winning football games.

Nearly every news reporter and blogger reported that Leach had won the negotiations; some compared it to calling the university's bluff in a poker game and then rolling over the winning hand. The Tech good ole boy titans of academia, business, and law—along with the small clique of large donors—had been bested, and they were likely embarrassed and unhappy. Not getting their way was bad enough, but being beaten by city slicker Yankee agents and a quirky pirate made it all that much more humiliating. As solace, many kept in mind Jim Sowell's email of December 30, 2008 where he wrote, "I feel you should sign a contract that would not cost us too much to fire him." They would wait, at times not all that patiently, to gain their apparent revenge and restore their collective good ole boy, West Texas honor.

On February 20, 2009, the day after Leach signed his new contract, Board Member Jerry Turner emailed Sowell and Anders. He wrote, "We might have a lawsuit, but if we fire him on November 30, 2009, the contract does not entitle him to receive the completion bonus." In this statement, Turner was in error. The actual date that Tech could fire Leach and avoid the completion bonus was December 30, not November 30, 2009.

Chapter 8

The Magic Continues
–The 2009 Season

Except for a few disgruntled administrators and regents, the citizens of the Red Raider Nation were happy to get the contract negotiations behind them and to get on with the preparations for the 2009 season. After nine years of Tech football victories under Leach's leadership, the fans had grown to expect a winning season and an invite to a bowl game. Leach and his team were ready and willing to do their best to make it happen once again.

Several things stood in the way, however. The prolonged, often adversarial, contract talks seemed to have damaged Leach's recruiting efforts and even impacted his coaching staff. A few athletes who favored Tech—and who would have been a good fit for Leach's offense—looked elsewhere when it appeared that the coach either might not return or possibly end up a lame duck without a long-term contract. Emory Blake, a top-ranked receiver from Austin, visited Tech at the end of the 2008 season, but he committed to Auburn University in January 2009 when the Leach contract negotiations stalled.

Contract negotiations also impacted Leach's assistant coaches. Unsure of their boss' stability—as well as their own—some looked for other positions. Seth Littrell, running-backs coach and one of Leach's best recruiters, departed for a similar position at the University of Arizona in February. Both Blake and Littrell credited the contract problems with their decisions to go elsewhere.

Even if these problems had not existed, no one really expected the Red Raiders to match their successes of 2008. The best season in the team's history with an 11-2 record and a flirting with the number 1 National Rating just was not going to happen again. All of the pre-season analysis emphasized Tech's difficulties in replacing the dynamite trio of quarterback Graham Harrell, receiver Michael Crabtree, and defensive end Brandon Williams. Despite these personnel losses, sportswriters had developed a respect for Leach and his brand of football and predicted that the Red Raiders would still play an important role in deciding the Big 12 South.

Nathan Lusk, writing in the bleacherreport.com blog about the personnel losses, echoed the sentiment, "Because of Mike Leach's leadership and creative play making and play calling, these setbacks [contract delays] will slow down the Red Raider offense, but they will still challenge for leadership of the Big 12 South."

Despite the confidence in Leach and the Red Raiders, sportswriters were also well aware of the strength of the other Big 12 South teams. The pre-season Associated Press Poll had Texas, Oklahoma, and Oklahoma State in its Top 10. Tech received votes but not enough to break into the Top 25.

Expectations for Texas Tech to finish high in the national ranking may have been absent, but a huge national interest in Red Raiders football still prevailed. The 2008 Tech-Texas game had earned ESPN its highest rating for the season and the fourth highest in the network's coverage of college football. ESPN, partnered with ABC Television, wanted the same lineup for another, earlier game for the 2009 season and began their plans early. When they saw that both Tech and Texas had open dates on September 19, they opened talks with the two universities and the Big 12 to reschedule the rematch slated for November 7. On February 10, ABC announced the change of the game date and began early promotion preparations for what they billed as one of the key matchups of the year and best of the early season games.

Tech opened the 2009 season at home against North Dakota. The Red Raiders scored on their first possession and went on to lead at half time 21-6. In the second half Tech gave up a single touchdown while adding 17 points to their winning total of 38-13. Junior Taylor Potts, the new Tech starting quarterback, completed 34 of 48 passes for 405 yards as the Tech offensive machine continued its tradition of many yards gained and high points scored.

Week Two pitted Tech against their former Southwest Conference rival Rice University. The Red Raiders scored at will against the hapless Owls, winning 55-10. Potts tossed seven touchdown passes while his backup Steven Sheffield, also a junior, added another.

When Tech met Texas on September 19 at Darrell K. Royal Memorial Stadium in Austin before a crowd of 101,297, the Number 2 ranked Longhorns were a huge favorite. The unranked, underdog Red Raiders stayed close in the first half, going into the break trailing 10-3. They matched the Longhorns with two touchdowns each in the third quarter only to be outscored 10-7 in the fourth for a losing final score of 34-24.

On Week 4 the Red Raiders faced another Top 25 team, again on the road. The 23rd ranked Houston Cougars fielded a pass-oriented offense similar to that of the Red Raiders, but the game proved to be surprisingly low-scoring—at least for these two teams. Tech led at the half 21-13 and at the end of the third 28-23. With seven minutes left in the game, Houston held Tech on a fourth and inches at the goal line. Then Houston marched down the field for a touchdown with 49 seconds remaining. Tech could not mount another score before the gun went off, sealing a 29-28 Cougar victory.

Tech's final non-conference game ended with an easy victory over New Mexico by 48-28. Taylor Potts led the Red Raiders to score in their first possession but went down with an injury in the second quarter. He did not return to the game. Sheffield stepped in to throw a touchdown pass in the second and two more in the third quarter.

In their homecoming game against Kansas State, Tech got back on their high scoring, crowd-pleasing pace. Earning at least two touchdowns in each quarter while allowing the Wildcats only two total scores, Tech easily won 66-14—the most points ever scored against a team coached by legendary Bill Snyder.

Tech was back before a national ABC television audience of more than 86,000 fans at Memorial Stadium in Lincoln, Nebraska on October 17. The Tech defense kept the favored, 15th ranked Cornhuskers in check while their own offense continued to score. After the victory of 31-10, Tech—now 5-2—moved into the Top 25 for the first time in the season.

The next game appeared to the odds makers to be an easy choice. Tech had beat Kansas State 66-10. Kansas State whipped Texas A&M 62-14. So when Tech faced the Aggies, the question did not seem to be who would win but rather by how many points. Potts was back at quarterback after an injury put Sheffield on the sidelines in street clothes. When Potts faltered, Leach put in Seth Doege, a redshirt freshman and Tech's third quarterback of the season.

Tech led 14-7 at the end of the first period but over the next two quarters A&M scored 31 unanswered points before the Red Raiders got back on the board. A&M scored twice more in the fourth quarter against a single touchdown by Tech to win 52-30. In his postgame interview Leach said his team was overconfident and that his players had been listening too much to their "fat little girlfriends" who destroyed their mental edge by telling them how good they were. The defeat cost Tech its national ranking; the comment cost Leach a few fans, at least temporarily.

Tech hosted Kansas on October 31 at Jones Stadium. Doege got his first start because Potts and Sheffield were still recovering from their injuries. The teams were tied at the half at 14-14 and then the Jayhawks took a touchdown lead in the third quarter. Tech scored four unanswered touchdowns in the fourth to win 42-21.

Potts and Sheffield returned for the next game against Oklahoma State and shared time quarterbacking. The Cowboys, at number 18 nationally, were focused on improving their rankings while avenging their 56-20 defeat the previous year. Tech's defense bottled up the Cowboy's vaulted ground game in the first half, but the Red Raiders went into halftime with only a 10-7 lead. In the second half the Oklahoma State running game ate up yards and time while their defense intercepted three Tech passes to outscore the Red Raiders 17-7 for a final victory of 24-17.

The next game on the schedule offered the opportunity for Tech to settle old scores from the previous year. In the Golden Season of 2008 the University of Oklahoma Sooners had burst Tech's bubble of national champion hopes. Tech got their revenge in the Magic Season of 2009. With Potts back in charge, the teams were tied with a field goal each at the end of the first quarter. Then the Tech offense began to light up the scoreboard while the Sooners did not score a touchdown until the game's last minutes. Final score was in favor of Tech 41-13.

The following week Tech opposed Baylor University, which should have been an easy win. Baylor at 4-7 was having a bad year, and almost everyone thought Tech would end the regular season with an easy victory. But as Leach had noted, 'We don't seem to put two good games together in a row.'

Such was the case in the match up played in the new Dallas Cowboy Stadium before a crowd of nearly 72,000. Baylor led at the half 10-3 and then 13-3 in the third before Potts threw for two scores to put Tech ahead 17-13. In the fourth the Red Raiders added a field goal only to have to hold the Bears four times inside their own ten yard line to preserve the 20-13 victory.

The 2009 regular season record of 8-4, of course, did not meet the bar of success and excitement that the Golden Season of 2008 had set. However, the magic had allowed the Red Raiders to defeat two ranked teams and earn themselves a bid to the Valero Energy Alamo Bowl—and its $2.2 million payout. And they had won eight regular season games while having to start three different quarterbacks because of injuries. In his nine previous seasons, Leach had not had a quarterback miss a single start because of an injury. Contrary to preseason predictions, the Red Raiders had once again overachieved.

Leach's legion of fans continued to grow. On December 3 a group of supporters from Houston surprised Leach at the end of a team meeting in Lubbock to honor him for achieving the most wins of any football coach in Texas Tech history. The supporters also noted that it had taken Leach three fewer years to set the all-time wins mark than it had the previous record-holder Spike Dyke. They presented Leach with an engraved Rolex watch, a heavy double T emblem fashioned from aerospace aluminum, and a 30-inch stainless steel replica of a pirate sword. As the fans and the coach celebrated the benchmark, little did they know or suspect that Leach was about to sail into rough waters where new opponents and old enemies would unite to try to sink the old pirate and to destroy his meteoric career.

Leach set book signing records in Lubbock and out drew Sarah Palin and Colin Powell at a bookstore in Dallas

Leach's *Swing Your Sword* was co-written with Bruce Feldman, who left ESPN after a long career as a college football writer, when he was suspended shortly after the release of *Swing Your Sword*.

The beautiful English Philosophy Building at the Texas Tech University Campus.

West side of Jones AT&T Stadium, home of the Texas Tech Red Raiders football team.

Clock Tower at Texas Tech University Campus
Photo Credit: Andrew Allbritton

AT&T Jones Stadium, looking at the new press box, luxury suites and new end zone seating built in response to the huge fan support generated by coach Mike Leach.
Photo Credit: Andrew Allbritton

Students with the Guns Up during the school fight song.
Photo Credit: Nicholas Moore
Shuterstock.com

Tech students getting to the stadium early with their Raider Power Banners.
Photo Credit: Andrew Allbritton

Students doing their Guns Up salute to the football team. The Guns Up is the hand signal used by the Tech faithful.

Photo Credit: Andrew Allbritton

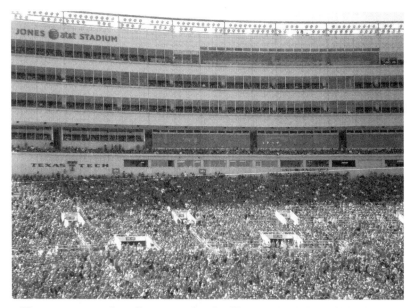

The new press box/luxury suite facility on the West Side AT&T Jones Stadium. Included in this is a large Chancellor's Suite, stocked for special guests to enjoy during the game.

Photo Credit: Andrew Allbritton

Danny Amendola – Wide Receiver
Photo Credit: Nicholas Moore / Shuterstock.com

Graham Harrell – Quarterback
Photo Credit: Nicholas Moore / Shuterstock.com

Coach Leach on the sidelines with Seth Doege–Quarterback.

Kent Hance (black hat) observes a conversation between Coach Leach and former Head Coach Spike Dykes.

Coach Leach in action. Making it happen!
Photo Credit: Andrew Allbritton

Coach Leach on the screen.
Photo Credit: Andrew Allbritton

Craig James
Photo Credit: Vince Swagerty

Chapter 9

The Phony Express:
Craig and Adam James

Craig James set records his entire football career. At Stratford High School south of Houston, he claimed the single-season Texas 4-A rushing record in 1978 with 2,411 yards. At Southern Methodist University (SMU) he teamed with Eric Dickerson to form the top rushing duo in the nation in what became known as the Pony Express, a word play on the SMU Mustang mascot. In the 1980 Holiday Bowl, James set rushing and yards-per-carry records that stood for more than a decade. Two years later he caught a pass for a 96-yard touchdown—the longest scoring play in Southwest Conference history.

When James played with the New England Patriots, the Vince Lombardi Committee named him the "Offensive Player of the Year" for 1985. That same year James was a starter both in the Pro Bowl and in Super Bowl XX.

But those were not the only records attributed to James. He still holds other records—though two are of a dubious nature. He is the only individual in more than a century of gridiron history to have a primary role in tarnishing the football programs at two major universities. First, James, as a part of the Pony Express, played on SMU teams where individual payoffs and other National Collegiate Athletic Association (NCAA) violations were routine, resulting in the Mustangs' being the only college football program to receive the NCAA "Death Penalty"—a penalty so severe that it virtually kills a college football program for years, if not decades. Second, a quarter century later James provided the information, influence, pressure, and public relations campaign that contributed significantly to the firing of Mike Leach at Texas Tech University.

When James joined the SMU team in 1978, the Mustangs had one of the most celebrated programs in college football, having garnered a national championship, a Heisman Trophy winner, and 10 Southwest Conference titles. In his senior year, James and Eric Dickerson led SMU to an undefeated season. Between 1980 and 1986 the Mustangs compiled a record of 52-19-1.

Unfortunately, SMU did not always play by NCAA rules, and this was especially true during James' years as a Mustang. When they were placed on three years' probation in 1985 for recruiting violations, SMU had already been on probation seven times, five of those times in the previous 11 years—more than any other Division I-A school.

The 1985 probation was based on evidence that players were being paid what amounted to cash salaries along with their receiving other unauthorized benefits. SMU promised to end the payments, but the school's board of governors decided that they had an obligation to honor previous payment commitments to their players.

In 1986, WFAA Television of Dallas-Fort Worth and *The Dallas Morning News* revealed that players were still being paid through a slush fund supported by wealthy boosters. A subsequent NCAA investigation found that 13 players had received $61,000 ranging from $50 to $750 per month. The NCAA imposed what the press labeled the "Death Penalty" canceling the SMU 1987 season and its home games in 1988, extending the probation sanctions until 1990, dropping 55 new scholarship positions, lowering the number of authorized assistant coaches from nine to five, and limiting off-campus recruiting until the 1988 school year.

After handing out the harshest penalties in college football history, the NCAA Infraction Committee stated that the violations had given "great competitive advantage" to SMU and that the committee had been forced to "eliminate a program that was built on a legacy of wrongdoing, deceit and rule violations."

Since 1989, SMU has won fewer than a third of its football games. Only in the past several years has it returned to a competitive level. In addition to the Mustangs' own demise, the scandal also harmed the finances and reputation of the Southwest Conference, contributing, in part, to its end in 1996.

While Craig James was a member of the "pay for play" teams for his entire tenure at SMU, he was not listed as one of the 13 salaried players in the investigation. He denied then, and continues to deny today, that he participated in the payments. He did admit, however, while under oath in his sworn deposition on March 13, 2010, "I never accepted anything from an SMU administrative official, but I was 18 or 19 years old, and you know, I'm not going to say that I didn't take 20 or 50 bucks at a party if a booster came up to me."

What James did not point out was that "50 bucks" in 1985 money is worth about $104 today, making that amount more tempting than it might have sounded initially, nor did he mention how many "parties" he attended. He also made no comment on how much his own success—and resulting generous NFL contract— was influenced by "pay for play" linemen and others who contributed to his on-field success. Whether James personally avoided the graft of regular salary or if he simply sold out cheaper than his teammates remains an unanswered question.

While SMU struggled for years to recover from its Death Penalty, James had a financially lucrative and successful professional career before retiring after the 1988 season. In 1989 James went to work as a sports anchor for KDFW Television in Dallas-Fort Worth and as a radio commentator for SMU football games. He also appeared as a studio analyst on ESPN's *College GameDay* and *College Football Scoreboard.* In 1993 James established the Craig James School of Broadcasting that specializes in training former players for on-the-air jobs.

In 1996 James jumped to CBS where he performed as a studio analyst on their *College Football Today* and *NFL on CBS* programs. While at CBS he also covered the NCAA Basketball Championship and the 1998 Winter Olympics. Craig James moved to ABC as a studio analyst for college football in 2003 and also resumed his appearances on various ESPN shows. In the

2009 season he began work as a game analyst for ESPN college football matchups telecast on ABC.

James and his wife home-based their family first in the Dallas suburb of Addison, where their children attended private school, before they relocated to Celina, a small town about half-way between the Metroplex and the Oklahoma border. At Celina High School, one of the traditionally top football 4-A schools in Texas, James' son Adam joined the class of 2006 and started his last three years as a tight end there. According to the Texas Tech web site and his own claims, Adam received scholarship offers from Tulsa, Boston College, and Wisconsin but decided to stay closer to home and attend Texas Tech. Some sources claim Adam did not receive any credible offers other than from Tech and that one came only after a lobbying effort on the part of his father. Neither James nor Tech has ever offered any proof that any Division I school other than Tech offered Adam a scholarship.

Not all the Tech coaches concurred with recruiting Adam James into the Tech program. Many athletes have the ability to play major college football; not all have the mental toughness, dedication, and persistence required to actually contribute to the team. Some are just not willing to do the necessary hard work. Adam James appeared to be one of them.

Dana Holgorsen, in an email supporting Leach after his termination, wrote, "I was the inside receiver coach at Texas Tech when we made the decision [to] sign Adam James in January 2007....After a conversation between Coach Leach and Adam's father Craig, Coach Leach acquired a brief highlight tape of Adam and made the decision to take him as a scholarship student athlete."

Holgorsen, who went on to be the offensive coordinator at the University of Houston and then head coach at West Virginia, continued, "I was opposed to doing so in (the belief) he was not a D I [Division I] player. Coach Leach overrode my opinion and Adam became a Red Raider. During the rest of my time at Texas Tech I was Adam's position coach where I always remained critical of Adam's ability to play at this level due to being lazy in not only the classroom but also in the offseason during practice."

Holgorsen continued, "Coach Leach was the one who kept saying he believed Adam would eventually contribute. Adam's teammates believed he was selfish and were constantly getting on him for lack of effort as they sensed entitlement on his part due to his father being a very good football player. Adam eventually ended up playing a little after I left due to his body type being able to do some TE [tight end] sets which consist of around 5-10 plays a game."

Holgorsen concluded, "Adam should be thankful for the opportunity to play at Texas Tech and for Mike Leach, who gave him the opportunity. In my opinion playing 5-10 plays a game in an outstanding offense is more than he would get at any other school in NCAA DI football."

Adam James arrived on the Tech campus in the fall of 2006 as a "gray shirt" freshman, meaning he was not yet on the team and had to work out on his own. He officially joined the Red Raiders as a redshirt freshman for spring drills in 2007 and then worked on the scout team. He became a part of the regular team for the 2008 season—so in essence James had five and a half years' potential association with the Tech team.

Throughout Adam's first two years at Tech, his father Craig was a regular on campus, attending practices and talking to the coaching staff. In his sworn deposition of March 13, 2010 the elder James stated he went "to some practices, a few" in the spring and then "six, seven, or eight" practices during the summer two-a-days. Craig James claimed that most of this attendance was in his role as an ESPN analyst and that he covered three Tech games. He admitted that he talked to Tech coaches about his son but denied that they discussed Adam's playing time.

Craig James stated in his deposition that he had also talked to Mike Leach at the practices. According to Leach, in one of their discussions James mentioned to him that he was in business with Chancellor Kent Hance in an apparent effort to influence the coach's future player decisions.

In an interview with the Associated Press on January 1, 2010, Leach said that Craig James lobbied frequently for more playing time for his son. The coach claimed that James meddled "more than any parent I've dealt with my entire career."

Leach continued, "I can understand a father being a fan of his son, being supportive of his son. But at some point coaches have to be allowed to coach. At some point the wisdom of all the people watching the film, going to all the practices has to be respected. Just because you have influence, power and a microphone in front of you doesn't mean that your son should have any more right to play than the other guys."

The elder James attended so many practices and made so many phone calls to the coaching staff that they soon began referring to him as a "helicopter dad" for the way he kept "dropping in and hovering." They also less politely called him a "junior high dad" and a "little league dad" because of his interference.

During the Golden Season of 2008, Adam James was played sparingly as a freshman and caught 15 passes for 159 yards and a touchdown. James continued to fail to impress his coaches with his work ethic in practice and in the classroom. Dennis Simmons, a recruiting coach also responsible for class checks, reported in the fall of 2007 that James had missed several classes and that the coaching staff had been receiving negative reports on his academic standing.

His fellow players also found fault with Adam. Eric Morris played inside receiver in the Golden Season of 2008 before graduating and going to the Canadian Football League as a free agent. Morris, now the offensive assistant at the University of Houston, later sent a "To Whom It May Concern" letter about James. He stated, "You can find out a lot about a person after playing three years of college football with them. Ever since the day he arrived at Texas Tech, you couldn't help but feel a negative energy from him. He expected people to baby him and that he was going to make it solely on the fact that his father was a very successful player. Adam was never known as a hard worker....he always seemed to have a negative attitude towards the football program the majority of the time."

In a similar email Graham Harrell, quarterback during the Golden Season, said that James had a negative impact on the team "because of his attitude and work ethic on and off the field." Harrell added that during off-season workouts James would skip reps in the weight room and was always trying to cut corners to get out of conditioning exercises.

Harrell also wrote, "When we had players organized seven on seven throwing in the summer, when he would show up, he was much more interested in playing his own game on the side of the field or telling people that he wasn't going to run any routes because the coaches did not give him a 'fair opportunity.'"

He continued, "None of these acts were productive for our team, but the most detrimental part of Adam was his off the field attitude and actions. In the locker room and away from the facilities Adam used any opportunity he had to tell other players that he was being treated unfairly...Adam pretty consistently talked bad about the coaches or down played the importance of working hard when he was off the field. When Adam talked to young players or players that were usually on the scout [team], he would explain how the coaches were not fair to certain players and only played favorites. Because of Adam's work ethic and attitude, many of the players on last year's team had a hard time trusting him or relying on him because he was not always practicing and we had seen his laziness during the off season."

In his sworn deposition Craig James was asked if he thought all of Adam's teammates were lying about his attitude and dedication. He responded, "Could be."

He was then asked if he believed that any of them was telling the truth to which he again answered, "Could be."

To the question about his son skipping classes, James said, "I think it's part of being a student."

On September 10, 2009 receiver coach Lincoln Riley, a former Texas Tech walk- on quarterback, called Adam James into his office. Riley showed him film displaying what the coach called "poor effort" and informed him that he was demoted to third team. James stormed out of the room screaming "Fuck you" in front of Riley, staff, and fellow players. He slammed the office door so hard he caused $1,100 in damages.

In his sworn deposition of March 13, 2010, James admitted to breaking the door but denied "cussing." He acknowledged that he did not pay for the damages to the door.

Adam texted his father shortly after leaving Riley's office, informing him that he had been demoted to third string and would "not be getting many reps this week." Craig James then called Tech Director of Football Operations Tommy McVay, telling him in effect, "you coaches are crazy and you're screwing my kid."

When he got no satisfaction from McVay, the elder James called Riley and left a message, stating, "You don't know what you are doing. Adam James is the best player at the wide receiver position. If you've got the balls to call me back, and I don't think you do, call me back." When asked under oath in a series of questions about this statement—if he had made the statement—James replied, "I may have. I may have." Then, "I could have. I could have." And finally, "I believe I could have, yes."

Coach Riley forwarded the voice message to Leach, who then called in Adam for a meeting. Leach asked Adam to have his father cease his calls to the Tech coaching staff. Adam apparently relayed the request because Craig James did stop his calls to the coaches. He did not, however, stop lobbying for his son. It appears that he soon began telephoning Chancellor Kent Hance, Regent Larry Anders and other school administrators to complain about Adam's lack of playing time.

Despite the attitude of the younger James and the interference of his father, the Tech coaching staff continued to work with Adam to make him a better player. They also played him on a limited basis in the 2009 season where Adam caught 17 passes for 154 yards and a touchdown. However, as the year wound down, the father-son team mounted what looked like one more assault against Leach and the Tech football team.

Chapter 10

The Garage, the Media Room, the Electrical Closet, the Lies

Post-season bowl games are always a dilemma for coaching staffs in that they are extremely difficult to prepare for. The games are rewards for a successful season and an opportunity for the players to be hosted and entertained by the bowl committees. But bowl games are also serious, as they are the last opportunity for a team to add to its win total, move up in the national standings, and attract new recruits for the next season. Complicating the matter is the fact that teams often have a month or more between their last regular season game and their bowl matchup, time filled with final exams and the many distractions of the holiday season. As the Red Raiders prepared for the Alamo Bowl in December 2009, they faced another threat—the Phony Express was riding again, this time in the form of Craig and Adam James, who were evidently out to trample Coach Mike Leach.

The coming maelstrom began routinely enough. On December 14, 2009 during the first period of post-season practice for the Alamo Bowl, Leach counseled Adam about his sub-par effort and told him if it continued he would be sent to "Muscle Beach." This area, overseen by strength coach Bennie Wylie, included weight lifting equipment and devices used by injured players to help speed their recovery and to allow them to continue to be able to exercise. It was also used as an area for additional sprints, stair climbs, and other drills intended to motivate players lacking in focus.

During the second period of practice, Leach advised James and two other players that their efforts were unacceptable. He sent them to Muscle Beach where Wylie put them through remedial exercises that included running and stair climbing. Upon the completion of the drills, two players admitted to Wylie that they had, in fact, been deficient in practice and had learned from the discipline session; they promised to work harder in the future. The third player, Adam James, allegedly told Wylie that the coach did not know what he was doing and that his own personal effort in practice had been satisfactory.

Long after evening practice at about 10:45 p.m. on the evening of December 16, Adam James reported to athletic trainer Mark "Buzz" Chisum that he had been hit by a defensive player late in the scrimmage that day and that he was not feeling well. Chisum reported in his affidavit of April 23, 2010, "[Adam] stated that he was feeling dizzy and disoriented and that he had blurred vision."

Chisum administered a written Sports Concussion Assessment Tool (SCAT2) and determined that James's symptoms "were consistent with an athlete who has a concussion." The trainer then told James to take Tylenol for pain or for a headache and to call him if his symptoms got any worse.

The next morning James reported to the training facilities where he was seen by head trainer Steve Pincock and Doctor Michael Phy, who worked in the Texas Tech Health Science Center and was one of the physicians for the football team. Dr. Phy conducted his own tests and diagnosed him with a "mild concussion." Phy then recommended that James not practice for the next seven days.

Interestingly, concussions had recently become a "hot topic" with the NCAA and had been in the news for several weeks prior to the James incidents. A *New York Times* article on November 18, 2009 reported that the NCAA was concerned about concussions, though they were still leaving management of such injuries to the colleges. According to the article—which was replete with discussions of symptoms and side effects—the NCAA wanted each school to establish its own protocols and procedures concerning concussions suffered by student athletes.

The two initial primary witnesses to the concussion claim— Head Trainer Pincock and Dr. Phy— took Adam's complaint at face value and treated him accordingly. Little did they know how important each of their actions surrounding the injury would become.

This is the point in the storyline where the plot fractures and what happened next depends on who is telling the tale—and when. What all agree on is that Adam was diagnosed with a "mild concussion" by Dr. Phy, that the doctor told him to avoid workouts for seven days, and that Adam showed up for football practice on the afternoon of December 17 twenty minutes late wearing street clothes, sun glasses, and his baseball cap on backwards rather than in a practice jersey and cleats, the uniform that even injured players normally wore. Head Trainer Steve Pincock reported that Adam displayed "an attitude" as he walked the field that day and that Mike Leach was not pleased to see him—injured or not—out of uniform and wandering around while his other players worked out.

Essentially what occurred next was that Adam James was escorted to a nearby building on the field that was about the size of a one-and-a-half-car garage to both get him out of the practice area and to afford him a dark place where the light would not bother his eyes, a normal treatment for concussions. The team did not have a scheduled practice the next day, and when Adam showed up the following day, December 19, he was escorted to another facility for the same reasons.

The actions of Leach and Pincock—both of whom were focused on preparing the team for the upcoming bowl game—on these two occasions were non-noteworthy and would likely never have been given a second thought—except that Adam James was the son of Craig James, and Craig James was armed with microphone access to a national audience via ESPN.

According to his own words, Adam found the idea of being placed in the first building "humorous" and texted his father about it from his cell phone. He claimed he was "locked in" the building, which, as it turned out, did not have any functional locking devices. When he received the text, Craig James was not amused—not in the slightest. His first reaction was to text his son back to ask what Adam would "allow" him to do about this. When the second incident occurred on the 19th and Adam sent him a video from his cell phone showing himself in an "electrical closet," the elder James evidently made plans to publically air his outrage, condemning Mike Leach and Texas Tech for putting his son in a potentially dangerous situation.

It was at this point that Craig James appears to have unleashed the full fury of his frustration that had built up over the time that Tech had denied the talent of his son and deprived him of his rightful playing time. Within twenty-four hours, James activated his public relations firm to assist in what would become an all-out assault on the coach. This was only one front of the blitz coming at Leach. Once the James accusations became public, the actions of Leach, Pincock, and Phy on December 17 and 19 took on a life of their own and played right into the hands of the Chancellor and his colleagues, the second front aiming for the coach.

In an attempt to have the events of the incident recorded as accurately as possible while still in the forefront of the participants' memories, the football staff had Pincock and Phy prepare written accounts. These statements, perhaps the most honest and least tainted by outside influences, were secured by the *Dallas Morning News* and published on January 2, 2010. In his statement made on December 25, 2009, Dr. Michael Phy wrote, "I saw Adam James as a patient on December 17. At that visit I diagnosed him with a mild concussion. I made recommendations regarding level of activity and treatment. These were shared with Adam and the athletic training staff and are documented in Adams' medical record. I was not aware of any incident until I was contacted by [Tech representative] Charlotte Bingham. She provided details of a complaint, and I completed a short phone interview and answered questions for her. According to the information given to me, no additional risks or harm were imposed on Adam by what he was asked to do."

On December 31, 2009 Head Trainer Pincock offered his statement, "In regard to Adam James situation, the first building was an athletic training storage garage, two of which were adjacent to the football field. Adam was placed in the sports medicine garage, there is no lock on this building. Normally, injured players are asked to perform exercises, however Adam could not participate in these drills, and was originally asked to walk around the field during practice. Adam showed up to practice in street clothes, no team gear, and dark sunglasses. Adam walked about 40 to 50 yards, very slowly and with a non-caring attitude. Coach Leach noticed Adam's poor effort and non-team attire, and asked that Adam be placed in a location where sunlight could not bother him as he was wearing sunglasses. Two trainers, including myself, monitored Adam at all times. I instructed Adam to stay in the garage and out of the sun, so the light would not worsen his condition. While in the garage, Adam was walking around, eating ice, sitting on the ground, and, at one point, sleeping; at no point was there any enforcement to make Adam stand up. Adam was checked by doctors every day.

"On the second occasion, practice was in the stadium, and Coach wanted Adam to be in a dark location to help his concussion and wanted him out of public view because of his poor attitude and bad work ethic. Zach [Zane] Perry, our equipment manager, suggested using the visiting team media room. I walked Adam to the room, which was as least as big as a two-car garage. Inside the room is an electrical closet. I looked in the closet and stated that there was 'no way Adam would be placed in there.' I shut the door to the electrical closet, and it was never opened again. At no time during the practice was Adam ever placed in the electrical closet. The door to the media room was never locked, and trainers attending to Adam stated that he was sitting at times during the practice. Adam was never locked in any facility, and was never placed in an electrical closet or tight space, or instructed to do so."

Pincock concluded his December 31 statement saying, "I received calls about both incidents from Charlotte Bingham, and was asked and answered questions on the subject, and pictures were taken of both locations. Adam exhibited no symptoms of a concussion after the first day; no memory loss, no confusion, and no dizziness."

Tech officials and Spaeth communications immediately began emergency actions and damage control to counter the original statements by Phy and Pincock. On January 1, 2010, Phy and Pincock were called in to make additional statements. The obvious influence of being questioned by their employers and with Leach already terminated was compounded by what appears to be Merrie Spaeth's providing input to the statements.

Phy added little other than to say, "In spite of the fact that James may not have been harmed by these actions, I consider this practice inappropriate, and a deviation from the medical standard of care."

Pincock's statement of December 31, that had reporters and bloggers saying it called Adam James a liar, was significantly changed and added to in the January 1 record. In his second statement Pincock said that on December 17 Leach had used extremely crude language about James and had directed that he stand in a dark place for the entire practice and that he wanted him to be uncomfortable. Pincock in his second statement confirmed that he told James not to go into the electrical closet but added that the media room was extremely cold.

Evidence that much of Pincock's amended second statement may have been influenced by Spaeth is revealed in her email exchange with Sally Post, Tech's Senior Director of Executive Communications. It is also significant that subsequent emails note Pincock's initial reluctance to sign the statement at all. Finally, it should be noted that just as there are only 120 head coaching jobs in Division I football, there are only 120 Head Trainer positions. With Leach already gone, Pincock would have to have been concerned about his own employment future.

Adam James' recollection of the period of December 16-20 is included in his sworn deposition of March 13, 2010. Early in his sworn statement it was established that James was 21 years old, to be 22 in February, at the time of the December incidents. He was not a teenage player despite his being only a sophomore by eligibility because of his previous gray- and redshirt season. Some of his testimony is in agreement with the statements and affidavits of Pincock and Phy, but parts of his rendition differ considerably.

James confirmed that he had been injured during practice on December 16, but he disputed that he had shown up in the improper attire on the 17th, as claimed by Pincock and Chisum. He admitted to eating ice, sitting down, and leaving the garage to use the bathroom. He said he had used his cell phone while in the training garage; but he insisted that he was "locked" in the shed despite it having no lock, and that he was not aware of anyone checking on his welfare every 15 minutes.

When asked if Pincock was lying in his statement that "at no point was there ever any enforcement to make Adam stand up," James responded, "I wouldn't say lying but I would say—I would say I don't agree with that." James added later that he would not call anyone a liar, but that he would say Pincock was "misinformed."

Adam James also admitted to texting his father from the training garage. The text began, "You're going to like this."

When asked just what he meant by this statement, James responded, "Well, we have the same sense of humor and personality and I thought—we thought it was funny. So I said 'you're going to like this.'"

When asked if he was having fun while composing the text to his father, Adam James said, "I wouldn't say having fun, but I did find it humorous."

Adam then confirmed that in his text he told his father that he had suffered a concussion the previous day and could not practice. He further texted, "Leach thinks it's impossible for me to have one and I'm just being a pussy."

When asked if Leach had ever told James he wanted him to practice with the concussion, he answered, "Well, no, he never personally told me, no, sir." He added, however, that that was the impression he got from Pincock.

When asked if he could provide even one piece of evidence or confirmation to support the claim that Leach wanted him to practice with a concussion, James answered, "I don't remember, but obviously I had some." He added that there was nothing, however, that he "specifically remembered."

In the text to his father, James had written, "So for punishment he had me locked in a pitch black shed for the whole practice." When queried about that statement, James responded it was accurate except for the first several minutes of practice when he was on the field. A lengthy question and answer session followed between James and attorneys with evidence presented that the garage was never locked and that, in fact, it had no operative lock. James maintained that he was locked in the shed, he said, "Because I wasn't able to leave."

James also continued to dispute claims that the trainers had checked on him every 15 or 20 minutes. When reread Pincock's statement to that effect and similar information noted in the findings by Tech investigator Charlotte Bingham, James was asked if he thought they were lying. He responded, "I wouldn't say lying, but I do not remember every 15 minutes the door opening." Of course, if he spent much of the time in the garage sleeping, it would have been difficult for him to know if anyone had checked on him.

In another portion of his text to his father, James had written, "If he catches me sitting down or leaning on the wall I'm kicked off the team." When attorneys asked if anyone had actually told him that, James responded, "Well, if I'm sitting here reading it, then obviously I mean I wouldn't have just made this up." Despite evidence offered that he spent the time in the garage eating ice, walking around, sitting, and laying on the ground, James continued to testify that those who had said he had misspoken about standing were wrong or misinformed.

When asked why he called the building a shed when everyone else referred to it as the garage or athletic training storage facility, James said, "Well, that's to me what it is, a shed." Yet, the so-called shed was familiar to all Tech players because it held the ice machine and served as a frequent "hang out" for offensive linemen during practice breaks.

James did not deny using his cell phone because the recorded time of the text message confirmed he sent it from the garage. His father texted him back asking, "Can you call me?" Adam responded, "no, just text."

When asked why he had said he could not call, James answered, "Because I was in a shed and there were people outside. And I wasn't supposed to be talking on a phone." James did not acknowledge that this was an admission of using his phone and confirmed that "people" were outside the garage.

Craig James texted back, "Call me when you can and think about what you will allow me to do." Adam responded, "Okay, I'll call you when I get out. Don't do anything yet though."

When asked why he told his father to not do anything, Adam said, "Well, because at the time I didn't want do anything. I had been put in a shed, and like I said earlier, thought it was kind of humorous." He later added, "I thought the idea of it was funny."

When he was asked why, since he had use of his cell phone, he did not call 911. James replied, "I wasn't in medical jeopardy."

The deposition continued to cover activities of December 18. James said that he went to the training facility but made no complaints about the previous day. He agreed that he still thought it was kind of funny and that he did not at the time view the incident "as any type of event that would or should lead to a coach being fired."

Throughout a lengthy question and answer period that followed about activities of December 19, James claimed that his impression from Pincock was that Leach wanted him cleared to practice despite his concussion. He finally admitted that there was nothing in Pincock's statement to support that accusation.

In response to questions about the period of time before and after he was in the media room, James claimed that Pincock told him that Leach wanted him "in the darkest, smallest, most claustrophobic space possible." He also said, "I believe he wanted me in a dark space. I don't know if it was necessarily to help with the concussion."

James added that the room was "possibly" as large as a two-car garage. He confirmed that the room contained an electrical closet, but he disagreed with Pincock's narrative and said he did not remember the trainer saying "there was no way that Adam would be placed in there" in reference to the electric closet.

James, however, testified that he believed Leach wanted him placed in the "electrical closet," and then when asked if he were ordered to be placed in the closet, said, "Under my assumption, yes." Despite this conclusion, James could not cite anyone as specifically saying that he should be in the electrical closet. He simply thought that is where they wanted him because it was "the smallest, darkest, most claustrophobic" space available.

In subsequent testimony James confirmed that Leach did not tell him to get into the electrical closet, but he continued to deny that he heard Pincock tell him not to. He admitted, "Nobody held my hand and pulled me in there." Yet he contended that when Pincock said "stay here," James understood the instructions to mean the closet instead of the media room where they were both standing.

Once left alone in the media room, according to his deposition, James let himself into the closet where he claimed he remained for about an hour. While in the closet he took a video of its interior with his cell phone—again admitting he knew it was against team policy to have in his possession at practice. On the video, James can be heard saying, "I'm going to turn the lights off-on real quick, I've got to be fast." He explained the need for speed, saying, "the lights were supposed to be off." James said he took the video to show his friends and "because it was bizarre."

The video—just 16 seconds in length—however, turned out to be the spark that lit the fuse that led to the biggest explosion in Tech football history. In the meantime, though, Leach had been fired and the administration was under siege.

When asked how the electrical closet video made its way to YouTube, James testified, "Mary (sic) Spaeth put it on there." He then equivocated, "I emailed it to somebody. Maybe her. I might have emailed it to her. I'm not sure."

In his testimony James confirmed his claim that he had heard

Leach, whom he said was in the hallway outside the media room—in spite of two closed doors separating them and buzzing background noise from the electrical equipment hissing in the closet—ask, "Is that motherfucker in there?" When told that Jordon Williams, the trainer who stood outside the media room had stated that Leach never made such a statement, James said, "I'm not aware of that."

Under direct questioning, James admitted that he was the source of everything his father knew about what happened on the 17th and 19th of December.

Craig James claimed the incidents had inflicted "great mental anguish" on his son. Adam agreed with that assessment and stated, "It's just I honestly feel like prisoner, a slave. I mean I don't think anybody wants to be locked in a closet, however you want to put it. It's just degrading."

When asked how he got out of the "locked" closet, James stated, "Myself." And as to how he got out of the "locked" media room, he responded, "I believe it was myself actually.…I realized practice was over, so I left."

James stated that he then went to the locker room but made no complaint to anyone in authority about his treatment. He also admitted that despite suffering "great mental anguish" that he never saw a psychiatrist or sought any counseling whatsoever.

There was also disagreement on the time James spent in the media room and electrical closet. During the one hour practice session, James claimed he remained in the electrical closet until he moved to the media room for the last "20, 30 minutes, maybe," explaining "because I was tired of being in the closet."

When confronted with the statement from Tech's own investigator, Charlotte Bingham, that Adam had told her he was in the electrical closet for only five minutes, Adam essentially called the attorney a liar when he claimed, "I did not tell her that."

Near the end of his testimony, James once again mentioned his complaint that he had been locked in the electrical closet and forced to stand on the orders of Coach Leach. He also reiterated that he had gone along with being locked in the storage shed and being forced to stand because of threats that he would be kicked off the team if he did not. He continued to testify that Leach had wanted him to attend full contact practice despite his concussion.

Mike Leach made his deposition on March 12, 2010. Early in the deposition, Leach was asked, "Do you, as you sit here today or at any time since then, feel you did anything wrong in your treatment of Adam James?" Leach responded, "No." When asked if he thought he owed the James family an apology Leach again answered, "No." He then confirmed that he had made previous statements that Adam James was lazy, that he had a sense of entitlement, wouldn't work hard, and he was always falling back on his father.

When asked about what happened on December 17, Leach said, "Well, we were bringing, you know, the team up, you know, just—practice had already begun. Adam James came slowly walking onto the field in street clothes, hat on backwards, head band on, sunglasses on. And I asked—and so I called Steve Pincock over, and I said—I said, why isn't he dressed? And Steve says, I don't know, he was late. And I said, well, what's he doing out here with sunglasses? And he said that his eyes are sensitive to light because he's got a concussion. And so I said, well, put him somewhere dark and have him do something."

Leach continued after being asked if he recalled anything else about the incident, "Well, I was upset that he—you know, that he basically had been a discipline problem and that he failed to follow the rules, you know. But—you know, and so then I swore in my frustration."

He then confirmed that he did not want a player loafing while other players were working out and again said that he had used cuss words on the field. He added that while Pincock had selected the garage for James, "I didn't really approve it, but after the fact I didn't have a problem with it." Leach also said that he did direct James to stand during practice, "because everyone else in practice was standing so I thought it was fine for Adam," but that he "never said anything about [James being] uncomfortable."

To the question as to whether having James placed in a dark place was therapeutic or punishment, Leach answered, "Well, really I think two things. He had been a distraction and was violating team rules, so I wanted him away from the team. And as far as the darkness, you know, he had overly sensitive parents [sic], so I wanted him out of the light. I wanted him somewhere where a ball or a body couldn't hit him and I wanted him somewhere he wouldn't exert himself to make sure that he was protected. But, you know, a portion of it is I wanted him away from the team because he was a distraction and defied team rules." He further explained he wanted James in a dark place, "Because his eyes were sensitive to light."

Leach then answered questions confirming that he never told Pincock to "lock" James anywhere and that Adam was never confined in a locked facility. He also stated that he did not recall ever calling Pincock to discuss James' concussion nor did he recall ever asking if Adam was faking the injury.

According to his testimony, Leach did not see James on December 18, but on the 19th Pincock approached the coach to ask what should be done with James at that day's practice. Leach said, "I don't know, whatever you did last practice is fine. And I don't know what happened initially. Then I went down the tunnel—because we practice on the game field instead of the practice field. As Jordon and I went down the tunnel Jordan said, Adam is in the media room. I said that's fine, and we went to practice." He then explained that the media room is about the size of a two-car garage "where we also put Mack Brown and Bob Stoops to do their press conferences after their games."

Throughout the remainder of his deposition Leach maintained that James had never been locked in any room whatsoever. He also maintained that James was placed in a dark room because of his sensitivity to light caused by his concussion, because he had not followed team rules, because he wanted to protect him from further injury, and because he did not want him distracting his teammates as they prepared for their bowl game.

Chapter 11

Preparing to Swiftboat Leach: Craig James and Spaeth Communications

Adam James may have found his time in the garage and media room to be "funny," but his father did not. Since the incident, Craig James has repeatedly stated that his only concern was for the safety of his son. His actions, however, indicate that he had an immediate but well-thought-out plan to smear Mike Leach and to secure his termination as head football coach of Texas Tech University. James was likely incensed over his son's lack of playing time; now it was time to get even.

On the evening of December 19, 2009, Craig James began his campaign, not by calling the coach or his direct supervisors—the athletic director, or the president—but instead by going to the university's Board of Regents. Larry Anders, Chairman of the Board, was in Austin for the wedding and reception for Governor Rick Perry's son when he received a cell phone message from his wife between the events. She said that mutual friends of theirs and the Jameses had contacted her to tell her that her husband needed to call Craig James in a matter of "life and death."

According to Anders' deposition of March 23, 2010, he had not previously spoken with James except when he briefly met him and they were able to "exchange pleasantries" at a fund raiser for the Governor the previous September. Nevertheless, he made the call between the wedding and the reception.

Anders stated in his deposition that in the first phone call, Craig James "was very upset that his son had been confined to dark rooms on two separate occasions, after having been diagnosed with a concussion." James also told him that Leach had placed Adam in an electrical closet, had used extremely profane language, and had intended "to humiliate and demean" his son.

Anders stated that he told James that Leach did not report to the Board of Regents and that they were not in charge of hiring or firing the football coach. Although there are some claims that James demanded Leach be fired in this first telephone conversation, there is no hard evidence that he did so until several days later. When Anders asked James if he had contacted Leach, he said he had tried but the coach would not return his calls. According to Anders, James said, "I'm through talking—trying to get ahold of Leach."

Anders then told James that he would report the incident to Chancellor Kent Hance, who was also attending the same festivities. Anders said he related the story to Hance during the reception. According to him, Hance then stepped outside and had a thirty to forty-five minute conversation on his cell phone with Leach.

In his deposition of March 11, 2011, Hance said that after a brief discussion of the incident, Leach told him that he intended to cut Adam James from the team after the Alamo Bowl. Hance appeared to want to settle the controversy as soon as possible, telling Leach, "You know, you got to work with me on this."

In the ensuing exchange they agreed on a course of action. According to Hance, "One is that you [Leach] will give him a release if he wants to transfer. Two, that he can stay on the team but y'all [James] got to quit calling and interfering. Or three, he can stay in school here."

Hance reported in his statement that Leach said, "We'll keep him on scholarship until the end of the year, until the end of May, May of 2010."

At no time in the telephone conversation did Hance order or request that Leach change his treatment of James. The Chancellor also reaffirmed that Leach was the person in charge of the football team. At this point, Hance should have turned everything over to the university president and the athletic director, but he did not. From the conversations and emails exchanged with current and past board members over the next few days, Hance apparently realized that he now had the ammunition needed to fire Mike Leach.

After the call, Hance told Anders that Leach's "account pretty well lines up with the allegations," though Leach later denied that he verified any of the allegations. Anders in his testimony added, "He [Hance] said…it's bad blood between the Jameses, and especially the dad."

When asked if at that time he believed the James version of the events were true, Anders answered, "That would be correct."

In his deposition Hance stated that he had first met James after the University of Houston football game the previous September. He said that James had mentioned that he was thinking of running for the U.S. Senate and asked if he could call sometime. Hance responded favorably and stated, "He'd call me up, I don't know, one or two times."

Later in the deposition the attorneys turned to the possibility of a business relationships' existing between Hance and Craig James. Following up on Leach's claim that James had told him that he and Hance were in business together, Hance was specifically asked if he or his family had any type of relationship with James. Hance responded, "No." When asked if Hance and any of the Jameses had been involved in a windmill farm together, again the Chancellor answered, "No." When asked if he knew the owner of ClubCorp, Hance said that the company was one of the groups that had the bid for concessions at Jones Stadium. When further queried if he had knowledge that the president of ClubCorp and James were SMU classmates, Hance said, "I did not know that."

After talking to Leach, Hance called Craig James from the Perry wedding reception and received the same basic report given to him by Anders. According to Hance's deposition, James expanded on his son's treatment. The Chancellor said that Craig James told him that Adam "had been put in shed or locked in a shed for two hours and then—two or three hours. And then the next practice was put in a dark room for two or three hours, not allowed to leave and was required to stand at all times." He added that James also claimed Adam had been "put in an electrical closet and there was buzzing and that he had to stay in this room."

When confronted at his deposition with the facts that Adam was not detained and that there were no locks as claimed by the elder James, Hance responded, "I think he misspoke on that."

According to the chancellor, the next day, December 20, he again called Craig James and outlined the three options he and Leach had agreed to for Adam, but he said that he found the sports announcer more interested in the past than the future. Hance recalled, "I think primarily he talked about that the treatment....[I]t was hard to keep him off of that subject and try to get him on something else."

The exact sequence and content of Hance's phone calls with Leach and James is difficult to pin down not only because there are no records of the conversations but also because of memory lapses. When in agreement with Anders and/or James, Hance's memory has remarkable detail. When asked about his conversations with Leach, however, his memory falters. In fact, in his deposition, Hance responded "I don't remember," or "I don't recall," or gave similar answers more than 35 times.

At this point Craig James must have understood that no matter how much lobbying he did, or how much he tried to influence the situation from behind the ESPN microphone, his son's playing days under Mike Leach were over. From existing records, exactly when James determined that, if his son was finished, then so was Leach cannot be pinpointed. But, according to his deposition, James had his lawyer hire the Dallas public relations firm Spaeth Communications "on or about December 23rd." It must have been more "on about" than "on" because, Merrie Spaeth, the owner of the firm and the one who billed James for their services, stated in an interview with Brooks Melchior of sportsbybrooks.com published on January 10, 2010, "I'm pretty sure his first call was on Dec. 19. He reached out to us." Other documents point to James retaining Spaeth as much as ten days earlier.

Spaeth added that James wanted her firm to, "help [the James family] with the first burst of attention. Our first role with them was to think through what to say publicly. We advised him on the drafting of the family's first statement that was distributed to reporters."

In his search for a PR company James solicited the top-of-the-line. Spaeth Communications, no stranger to national news and controversy, had "made a president" and been so effective in their efforts that the media had coined one of the most pejorative phrases of the early 21st Century to counter their claims—swiftboating.

Merrie Spaeth began her career as a teenage actress, her most significant role being in the 1964 film *The World of Henry Orient*. She left Hollywood to earn a degree at Smith College in 1970 and then another from the Columbia Graduate School of Business a decade later. In 1980 she became a White House Fellow at the Federal Bureau of Investigation, one of the first two women so chosen. After her stint at the FBI she served two years at the Federal Trade Commission as the director of public affairs and in 1983 President Ronald Regan selected her as the White House media relations director. She introduced the White House to satellite communications and launched its electronic news service. Spaeth is credited with moving the White House "into the Space Age."

In 1987, Spaeth founded Spaeth Communications in Dallas. As she put it, "Communication is the next frontier where business can gain a competitive edge. Most companies and individuals communicate what they want to say or what they think their audience needs to know. Spaeth Communications recognizes that communications should be treated as any other process—according to its impact on the target audience. This philosophy is the cornerstone of Spaeth's unique approach to communications."

One of Spaeth's more widely known quotations is, "We reinvent ourselves to solve a client's problem. It's more than just tweaking. It's rethinking what your audience wants and needs. Isn't that what great actors constantly do."

In 2004 the Swift Boat Veterans for Truth (SBVT) hired Spaeth Communications as their media representative to assist them in their opposition to the presidential campaign of John Kerry. Spaeth Communications helped the group of more than 250 veterans of swift boats—small, inland-waterway crafts used in the Vietnam War—navigate their protests against the candidate into attention-grabbing ads that claimed Kerry was exaggerating his service during the conflict. In these ads SBVT also challenged the legitimacy of Kerry's combat medals and claimed that Kerry had willfully distorted or withheld information about his own service as well as that of his fellow veterans.

And the Spaeth-assisted ads kept coming as the SBVT spokesmen declared Kerry to be unfit for the presidency and stated that his claims of atrocities and other war crimes by American servicemen and women who fought in Vietnam to be "a betrayal of trust." They showed clips of Kerry protesting the war by throwing away his medals, and they interviewed veterans who branded as lies Kerry's claims that he had entered Cambodian waters.

The liberal media skewered the SBVT ads as misleading and even false. But no amount of re-labeling and name-calling could sink the SBVT-Spaeth campaign. When they could not defeat or deflect the "swift boat ads," the pro-Kerry reporters and columnists turned the phrase into their own slam and began using it interchangeably with the term "smear campaign." Thus "swiftboating" became the pejorative term for any ad campaign that the liberal media does not agree with—despite the reality that the information contained in the SBVT ads against Kerry was based on historical facts.

The efforts by Spaeth Communications to get the SBVT message to the voters, whether it was the truth or merely a smear tactic, seemed to have worked. Kerry lost the election by a narrow margin.

The term swiftboating appeared again soon after the firing of Mike Leach. Within days of the announcement, web blogs such as sportsbybrooks.com, bleacherreport.com, and huffingtonpost.com ran articles titled, "Did Mike Leach Get Swiftboated at Texas Tech?" and "Swiftboating of a Pirate Captain."

While Spaeth Communications began preparing statements for the James family and planning its support campaign, Craig James continued his phone calls and emails to Chancellor Hance seeking action against Leach. Hance, instead of properly turning over the matter to President Bailey and AD Myers, began a dialog with Board Chair Larry Anders and Board Vice Chairman Jerry Turner while he made plans for his own investigation.

Only two days after the first Adam James incident, and on the day of the second, Craig James had created a triad of willing supporters in his apparent efforts to fire Leach. The first was James and his ESPN employer, the second Spaeth Communications, and the third Texas Tech University itself.

Chapter 12

The Investigation:
A Rush to Judgment

On December 20, 2009, the day after the second incident with Adam James and the telephone call from his father, Chancellor Kent Hance and Board of Regents Chair Larry Anders and Vice-Chair Jerry Turner met to discuss the problem. They faced several dilemmas.

First, they had to placate Craig James to prevent his bringing a lawsuit against Texas Tech. None wanted more bad publicity heaped on the university than James was already creating on ESPN. More importantly, the three were well aware that James had been selected to announce the upcoming Alamo Bowl—an additional forum in which he could embarrass Tech. While everyone was familiar with the phrase "the pen is mightier than the sword," the three men discussing the fate of Mike Leach were more than aware that the microphone and video camera trumped the pen and could easily bend or break the sword of the university and its football coach. The all-powerful, good old boys of West Texas were, in fact, somewhat intimidated by the nationally known sportscaster and the powerful television network he represented.

Second, the Chancellor and Board members knew that they had no authority to fire or take any other direct action against Leach. That responsibility lay with President Guy Bailey and Athletic Director Gerald Myers. Nevertheless, Hance, Anders, and Turner continued their involvement under the guise of what might be called "advisors" to the university's president and AD, by whom—unlike Craig James—they could not be threatened or intimidated. These three regents all had extensive experience in politics, business, and law. Turner also benefited from his time in the U. S. Navy, which provided him even broader leadership and supervisory experience.

In contrast, President Bailey had spent his entire career in the classroom and in the offices of the university administration. All of his accomplishments had been achieved in academia, including writing more than a hundred articles and books, mostly in the field of linguistics. Likewise, Athletic Director Myers had spent his career "on campus." His only work experiences were as a coach of teenagers and young adults and as the supervisor of other coaches. His bio always mentions that he still holds the second-best basketball free shot percentage record in Tech history. Neither Bailey nor Myers, despite being of age during the Vietnam War, had any military experience.

In the end, however, Hance and the board members had no doubts that the president and athletic director would do their bidding. Bailey and Myers were seemingly mere puppies in an environment ruled by wolves.

Third in the dilemma for the chancellor and his colleagues was that they wanted Tech to win the upcoming Alamo Bowl and to keep the fan base happy. With all their animosity toward Leach, they still recognized his coaching abilities and his importance to the team preparing for the big game.

The fourth factor—and the culminating one—was that Hance, Anders, and Turner recognized that they now had the justification needed to discipline, if not out-and-out fire, Mike Leach. Not only could they rid themselves of someone they appeared to personally dislike, but also his termination would open the door for them to hire an "our boy" who would treat them with the respect and deference they felt was due. More importantly, if Leach was no longer the coach on December 31, Tech would not have to pay him the $800,000 bonus due as a completion payment under provisions of the contract they had so opposed less than a year earlier. "Follow the money" is an old axiom—and an extremely accurate shortcut to the truth. Of all the factors, dollars held top priority to Hance and the Regents. The double cross, or maybe more appropriately, the multiple double crosses were about to begin.

After his meeting on December 20 with Anders and Turner,

Hance appears to have decided to exert his control of the situation by appointing one of his subordinates—rather than one of Bailey's or Myers' staff—to lead the investigation. Hance directed Charlotte Bingham, the vice chancellor of administration and managing director of the Office of Equal Employment Opportunity—and a University of Texas Law School graduate—as the investigator. Bingham, who had been in the position for nearly a year, had previously worked first in the local district attorney's office for five years and then for seventeen with a private law firm specializing in the defense of government entities and labor and employment law. Her ties and loyalty to Texas Tech are strong—and dual. In addition to her annual salary of $150,000, her husband is a professor in the university's chemistry department.

Bingham began her investigation immediately by interviewing Craig James that evening of December 20. According to her deposition of March 5, 2010, the elder James basically repeated his story about Adam's being confined and forced to stand in a shed and then in an electrical closet during two practices, though the elder James had no first-hand knowledge of the situations since he had learned everything he knew about them from his son. Bingham testified that James told her that "Mike needed to know that there would be consequences for his actions." She later added that James had said that if Tech "didn't address the situation, then he would get his legal team together and come down and depose people." When asked if she interpreted that to mean that he would sue the University, Bingham answered, "I did—I interpreted that as a threat of litigation."

Late on December 20, President Bailey decided to take a more active part in the investigation. He assigned Grace Hernandez, his chief of staff since his previous tenure at the University of Missouri-Kansas City, to assist Bingham and to monitor the interviews. Hernandez, who holds a masters degree in human resources, played little role in the inquiries except to observe Bingham's actions. She did not even write a report on the investigation. In her less than four-page affidavit given on April

10, 2010, she said little other than to support Bingham's findings.

In Mike Leach's sworn deposition of March 12, 2010, he testified, "I called Dr. Bailey [on December 21] and asked him what was the story with the investigation, and he said that he didn't think it was any big deal. He said, it's nothing to be alarmed about. They just want a paper trail of what's going on and that—but with that said between me and him he's going to send his assistant Grace Hernandez just to make sure that Kent doesn't try to railroad me because between me and him Kent has got a business relationship with Craig James. But he said he didn't see any real concern with it, and just give a statement and everything should move forward from there." Bailey later denied making these specific remarks to Leach.

Bingham, who never expressed any opinion about the addition of Hernandez, carried on with her inquiries the next morning, when she met Adam James at a coffee shop near the campus. In the one-hour interview, Bingham found that Adam's version differed markedly from that of his father's. (It also differed from Adam's own sworn testimony given later.) In the interview, Adam told Bingham that he was in the equipment shed on December 17 for one-and-a-half hours, was in the electrical closet for five minutes on December 19, and that he suffered no lasting effect from either confinement.

Shortly after her interview with Adam James on December 21, Bingham received an email, copied to President Bailey and AD Myers, from Board Vice Chairman Turner. The regent, again acting outside the guidelines of Texas Tech's own policies and those of the SACS, advised Bingham that the investigation could lead to the termination of Leach. Bingham admitted in her deposition that Turner was in violation of the Tech polices that "they [Tech] should follow it with regard to every employee."

For most of the rest of that day and on December 22, Bingham interviewed the other principals including Mike Leach, Steve Pincock, Buzz Chisum, Michael Phy, Tommy McVay, Jordan Williams, and Ted Liggett. She did not record the conversations nor did she have the interviewees prepare formal statements or affidavits. The details of her interviews come from her written report and her hand-written notes. During her deposition these sources would be supplemented by her memory of events.

By the afternoon of December 22, after only two days of interviews, Bingham considered her investigation into the Adam James incidents complete. At this point Bingham met face-to-face with Chancellor Hance, President Bailey, and AD Myers while Board Chairman Anders and Vice Chair Turner participated via a conference call. Interestingly, throughout the later depositions all the major participants are unsure if the meeting took place on the 22nd or 23rd. Documents support the 22nd.

Bingham presented her findings: (1) Adam James had a poor attitude both on and off the field and was a discipline problem; (2) James had broken an office door in a fit of anger about being moved to third team; (3) Craig James made repeated complaints about his son's playing time; (4) Adam James claimed to have a concussion and showed up at practice out of uniform and wearing sunglasses; (5) Mike Leach was concerned it would affect team morale if James was allowed to remain on the field; (6) Leach instructed his head trainer Steve Pincock to place James somewhere it was dark because he was sensitive to light due to the concussion; (7) Pincock selected the equipment garage; (8) James sat down, laughed, got ice, drank water while in the garage and left the building to go to the bathroom; (9) Neither Leach nor Pincock, nor anyone else ever ordered James to go into an electrical closet; (10) Neither Leach nor anyone else ever locked James inside any facility; (11) Assistant Trainer Jordon Williams confirmed that Leach never used profane language in front of James; (12) Williams was outside the garage and the media room to monitor James' condition; (13) James was not physically harmed or distressed by his treatment.

Despite her findings, according to her later deposition, Bingham still thought that some type of discipline should be imposed on Leach because "his actions were inappropriate and his unwillingness to address the manner in a positive manner" were unacceptable. Although she found that Leach never directed profane language directly at James during the incidents, she expressed concerns several times in her spring testimony about the coach's overall uses of obscenities.

During her deposition, Bingham was asked, "Did you ever recommend that Mike Leach be dismissed based on your investigation? She answered, "No."

Bingham's report was not well received by the administrators. According to Bingham and according to Hance's testimony in his deposition, Chairman Anders and Vice Chairman Turner stated that they still favored firing Leach. Both Anders and Turner denied making such a statement.

Turner, in particular, was concerned that Bingham did not gather affidavits from her interviews and asked her why they were not taken. According to Turner, Bingham, with an insight into how insignificant she thought the entire James controversy to be, responded, "Oh, we don't need them."

Bingham left for a vacation to Peru on December 27 and did not return to Lubbock until January 10, 2010. For two weeks her only contact with Hance and the other administrators was by telephone and emails and then only when, as she explained, she was not "out in the jungle."

When Bingham departed Lubbock for South America, she left no written report or other official documentation of her investigation. In an email to Hance, Turner wrote, "I can't tell you how upset I am that Charlotte said we don't need affidavits. And even after I strongly took issue with her, she didn't get any."

Despite Bingham's findings, by the 23rd it appeared that Hance had formally joined Anders and Turner in their opinion that Leach could be, and should be, fired. On December 26, Turner emailed Bingham, "Since this episode poses significant reputational risk to the University, I think it would be wise to assure the board knows the facts and has the opportunity to weigh in the manner to proceed."

On December 30, Bingham, now in Peru, received an email from Hance's office requesting a copy of her investigation report. When she responded she had not prepared one, Hance ordered,

"I need you to write a report of your investigation."

Bingham emailed a written report to Hance on December 31. The Chancellor then texted Bingham, stating, "The report is too mild. It needs the exact language and what Leach said about it."

A few hours later Bingham submitted an amended document only to receive another message from Hance telling her, "The report is too milk toast." As a result, the report underwent still more revisions, this time with input from Hernandez, Bailey, and Hance. Bingham justified this by stating that she did not have or remember all of the information she needed since she was away from campus and in Peru. In her deposition she also offered the excuse for the additions to and deletions from her initial report, saying, "I was writing them at night in a foreign country at a computer in a hotel. And I did the best I that I could with my recollection."

In the university's response to written questions about Bingham's report and findings, Chris Cook, the Texas Tech Director of Communications, provided little additional information. In his email he repeated that Hance put Bingham in charge of the investigation and that she had expressed concerns over Leach's behavior and language. Cook concluded, "At no time did either Ms. Bingham or Ms. Hernandez ever state that the investigation was no big deal."

In much of the conflicting testimony about the termination of Mike Leach there are "he said, he said," or in this case "he said, she said," statements with no witnesses, especially neutral ones, to validate the exchanges. Such is not the case in whether or not Bingham told Leach that the investigation was "no big deal."

In an article posted on *Texas Tech: The Official Web Site of Texas Tech Athletics* on November 16, 2001, Holly Krivokapich of the university's media relations office wrote, "Patty Ross has been as much of a part of Texas Tech football as Jones Stadium or Raider Red." That same Patty Ross was the Patty Ross, who was hired by Texas Tech in 1975 as a part of the ticket office, before she moved to the football staff a year later. At the time of Leach's termination, Ross had been the Senior Administrative Assistant to the head football coach for nearly 35 years. During that time she worked for six Tech head football coaches.

In an interview on September 13, 2011, Ross stated, "I sat in when Ms. Bingham talked with Mike Leach during the investigation. She told him that the investigation was 'no big deal' and that it was being conducted so 'some kind of paper' could be put in his file to close the case." When asked again to verify if she was sure she had heard Bingham say it was "no big deal," Ross responded, "Yes, that is correct."

In conclusion Ross stated, "I love Texas Tech and all the coaches I worked for. Mike Leach was always a gentleman and did great things for the team and the community."

Chapter 13

A Few Not-So-Good Men: The Rush to Firing

Despite the evidence presented by Charlotte Bingham that Craig James was incorrect in his accusations against Leach, regents Larry Anders and Jerry Turner left the meeting on the 22nd having recommended that Leach be terminated—an action they had evidently advocated since the contract negotiations of a year before. In the early evening of the 22nd, Hance, according to Leach's testimony, called the coach and informed him that "some members" of the board wanted to fire him as a result of the complaints made by Craig James about the treatment of his son. Hance did not explain just what Leach had done wrong but told him that some kind of disciplinary action, likely a fine of up to $100,000 and a demand for a letter of apology, would be initiated.

Leach responded that he had done nothing wrong and that an apology was not necessary. Hance ended the conversation by promising Leach that he would call again after he met with the Board of Regents. He never did. Rumors about the discussion between Hance and Leach being laced with profanities are denied by both men.

Hance never admitted it, but from all indications he had shared the desire with Turner and Anders to fire Leach ever since the contract talks. The university presents a united front still when asked, "What was the impact of the contentious 2009 contract negotiations in the ultimate firing of Mike Leach?" Speaking for Hance, Anders, and Turner, the university's Director of Communications Chris Cook, gives the official response in a single word, "None."

When the university was asked if Hance, Anders, and Turner were aware they would be in violation of Texas Tech policies and those of the SACS if they dealt directly with Leach rather than Bailey and Myers, Cook responded for them stating, "Chancellor Hance, Texas Tech Board of Regents Chairman Larry Anders, and Vice-Chairman Jerry Turner were advised and consulted regarding the matter, but the decision to terminate Mike Leach was made by President Guy Bailey upon the recommendation of Gerald Myers…We are unaware of any university or SACS policy that would prohibit the Chancellor or members of the Board of Regents from advising or consulting regarding allegations of mistreatment of a student-athlete by the Head Football Coach."

Meanwhile, President Guy Bailey and Athletic Director Gerald Myers, the two officials with the actual authority to terminate or otherwise discipline the coach, had reached a different conclusion. In his deposition, Bailey outlined his ideas for solving the problem. Bailey said, "If he [Leach] would accept from us a letter of instruction, if he would work with us on an apology or some sort of mutually agreeable response to the James family, I felt like we might be able to deal with the issue and get it behind us." Bailey added that issuing a suspension was "certainly not what I had decided to do."

Hance, Anders, and Turner met again on December 23. According to the chancellor, they discussed three options— reprimand, suspension, or termination. They seemed to have agreed that if they terminated Leach it would be for cause—thus nullifying their contractual responsibility to pay the upcoming $800,000 completion bonus.

However, the trio deny any relationship between the firing and the vast amount of money saved. A written question to Hance, Anders, and Turner asked, "Were you aware that terminating Mike Leach before December 31 would save the $800,000 completion bonus?" Again Cook answered for them. His email stated, "The issue was not discussed at the time, nor was it a factor in Gerald Myers' and President Bailey's decision to terminate Coach Leach."

On December 24, Chancellor Hance, emailed the two regents saying that he had given Bailey and Myers the authority to suspend or terminate the coach. Hance stated in his deposition that he came to that conclusion because Leach had placed Adam James in a dark place and told him to stand. He also said Leach was "insubordinate" and he was "just uncooperative. Wasn't going to work with us. Was going to do it his way. He didn't care what I suggested or anyone else suggested."

Despite the pressure from Hance, President Bailey and AD Myers did not move immediately to terminate Leach. Instead they prepared a letter to the coach about the inquiry with instructions on how they wanted him to treat injured student athletes in the future. The letter concluded with an admission that the allegations against Leach had not been confirmed but warned of various punishments, including termination, if they were verified (Letter at Appendix E).

The letter was dated December 23, but a blizzard sweeping through Lubbock was so severe that it prevented Bailey and Myers from presenting the letter to Leach until December 26. According to his deposition, Leach recalled, "At the meeting they presented me with a letter and asked me to sign it saying that they needed to put the letter in my file as part of the investigation. I told them that I was happy to cooperate with any part of the investigation, but I was not going to sign a statement that even remotely suggested I did something that I didn't. And I also pointed out that no portion of my contract suggests that I would have to sign such a document."

Bailey and Myers concurred that Leach was correct about his contract provisions but continued to encourage him to sign the letter. They also told him that Hance "really wants you to sign it" and that he "will be really upset if you don't sign it." They again told the coach that the letter was just for the files, but Leach still refused to sign.

Leach, Bailey, and Myers continued their dialogue for some time. The coach testified, " Because this thing had been going on for a couple of days, you know, with phone calls with Hance and investigations and the rest. So then finally I said, you know, if you don't want me here, just let me know. You know, let me know if you don't want me here. We can plan an exit strategy that will be beneficial to me; it will be beneficial to Tech; everybody will win on this thing. You know, publicity will work out excellent. We have a great recruiting class set up….We will have a great season next year."

Leach continued, "And then at the end of December, you know, we can work something out and agree that I will resign, and you can move on. And then, that way, you know, Tech looks good and that way we can have a successful season."

According to sworn testimony, Leach stated, "They said no, we are not interested in any exit strategy. This isn't about anybody losing their job and things like that. And they said that that's not what this is all about at all. This is not a big deal."

Apparently, Leach did indeed think it was "a big deal" and responded, "And I said—because it—it certainly began to appear that Tech was trying to fire me in order to—because in just a few days they owed me $800,000 in addition to other bonuses and things like that. And so is this—at the rate that this thing is accelerating and the rest it became, you know, fairly obvious that they were determined to fire me and that—and my position was, is it was to steal the money they owed me in the contract, in a contract that they probably weren't satisfied that they signed to begin with, but the public shamed them into it. And so my thought was an exit strategy that would be beneficial to everyone."

Again Bailey and Myers told Leach that they were not looking to fire him and did not desire an exit strategy. All they wanted was something in writing, not necessarily an apology, that would pacify the James family, Hance, and the regents so they could "get this thing behind us." Leach also testified that Myers said, "If Kent [Hance] would quit taking everything to the board and leave us alone, we could do our jobs."

Bailey, in his deposition, said that Leach was candid in the meeting with him and Myers. He also stated that Myers told Leach, "We wanted him to stay and be successful. We were not looking for termination of him."

When specifically asked, "So as of the 26th then in your meeting with Coach Leach, neither you, nor the athletic director, were thinking of terminating Coach Leach?"

Bailey answered, "That's right."

The meeting with Leach concluded without Bailey and Myers getting the letter signed, though in her role as the attorney for Texas Tech, Charlotte Bingham advised them that Leach did not need to sign the letter and that the letter could be placed in his file without his signature. At the same time, she told them that the James family should be called and told not to call again.

Bingham's advice about calling the Jameses was not heeded. Despite the conclusions and hopes of Bailey, Myers, and Bingham, the controversy was not going away. Craig James wrote Hance on December 26 demanding that Leach be fired. James again alleged that Leach had placed his son in an electrical closet—an accusation that by now only the elder James, and possibly Hance, Anders, and Turner still believed—or wanted to believe.

On December 27, before departing on her trip, Bingham left a voice mail for Ted Liggett, Leach's attorney, urging that the coach sign the December 23 letter because "outside pressures" were affecting the situation. She identified these pressures as the continued campaign by the James family to fire Leach.

Bailey and Myers, despite those "outside pressures" and their failure to get Leach to sign their letter of December 23, still favored keeping Leach as the coach of the Red Raiders. On December 27, Bailey and Myers prepared another letter for Leach, dated the 28th, that contained a "private reprimand," a fine of $60,000, and guidelines for the future treatment of injured players. Its last paragraph stated, "This concludes the inquiry into the allegations by Adam James and his parents."

Although Bailey and Myers were the only two individuals with the authority to present the letter for Leach's signature or to take any action against the coach whatsoever, they first circulated the draft letter to Hance, Anders, and Turner. The chancellor and regents apparently were not happy with the proposed course of action. They did not want to keep Leach—they still favored firing him.

Late on the evening of the 27th, Anders emailed Hance, writing, "I read the draft letter we discussed. I strongly urge you to not close this matter concerning Adam James with this approach. As I mentioned earlier today I don't want to eliminate our ability to use this to our advantage should we determine to use it to terminate Leach."

On the morning of December 28, Anders said the same thing to Bailey and Myers. These three, along with Hance and Turner, then again discussed the overall situation and appropriate actions. The puppies rolled over and let the wolves rule when Bailey and Myers evidently put their December 28 letter aside and acquiesced to Chancellor Hance, who declared that Leach had until noon that day to sign the letter dated December 23 presented to him on December 26 and a letter of apology to the James family. Otherwise he would be suspended. Unfortunately, no one told Leach or his attorney about the ultimatum or its deadline.

That same morning of December 28, while Hance and his allies were deliberating the coach's future, Leach and his Red Raider team boarded a plane and departed Lubbock for San Antonio to further prepare for the upcoming Alamo Bowl game on January 2. The Tech administration made no effort to have the coach remain on campus until the noon deadline. Instead, less than an hour after the team arrived in San Antonio, Myers called Leach to inform him that he was formally suspended from his coaching duties. The Athletic Director explained that the suspension resulted from an allegation against Leach for the mistreatment of a player and the coach's refusal to sign the letter of December 23, which Tech deemed to be an act of insubordination.

The obvious question for Myers and Bailey was "Why did you let the chancellor and board members take over the contract investigations and the James investigation when it was against Texas Tech policies and those of the SACS?" When the question was submitted through the university's Director of Communications office, spokesman Cook provided copies of the emails from Leach's agents noted in other places in this book.

He also stated, "The notion that Chancellor Hance took over the contract negotiations of his own volition is absurd."

Cook continued, "Leach's allegation that the Chancellor was looking for a reason to fire him has absolutely no factual basis."

Leach argued again that he had done nothing wrong. He also reiterated that not to sign a letter that contained inaccuracies was not being insubordinate. Myers told him that Chancellor Hance and the Board or Regents had made up their minds to suspend him and that there was nothing he could do to change the decision. Myers emphasized that Leach would not be coaching in the Alamo Bowl and that he was not to talk to the team members.

In one last attempt to reach a more compatible agreement, Leach, according to his deposition testimony, said, "You realize that, if you suspend me, it's going to be all over the media, and then I'm going to be very big publicity, and you and I are going to be right in the middle of it. So if we can come to a solution other than this, I think that's what would be best for everybody."

According to Leach, Myers responded, "They have already decided. There's nothing that can be done."

Leach was correct about the media interest in his suspension. In fact, his was the first and only story explosive enough to push the coverage of golfer Tiger Woods and his personal indiscretions off the front of the sports pages and TV shows.

The sports world was shocked; the Tech fans were incredulous; the general public, many of whom did not even follow college football, was intrigued that a bowl-bound university would suspend its winning coach, especially right before the game. The airwaves, presses, and keyboards went into meltdown. The country was riveted by the story.

As expected, reporters of all kinds descended on San Antonio and the Tech coach clamoring for details. Without reservation, Leach told his side of the events—much to the chagrin of Hance and his supporting regents and boosters—and emphasized that he had done nothing wrong.

While the world was shocked with what they had done to Leach, the regents were not yet done. Behind the cameras and in the background, the plot thickened when, on their behalf, Pat Campbell, General Counsel of Texas Tech, contacted Leach's attorney Tim Liggett and warned him that if he tried to interfere with the suspension Leach would be fired. This threat was in direct violation of Tech's own non-retaliation policy as well as provisions of its rules that allow aggrieved employees to remove a grievance to court.

Leach and Liggett did not back down. On December 29, Leach instructed Liggett to file a Temporary Restraining Order (TRO) to allow him to resume control of the team for the bowl game on the basis that the university had failed to accord the coach due process and that the university was in breach of contract.

Late that evening of December 29, Vice-Chair Turner emailed Hance and Anders to say that if Leach proceeded with the filing of his injunction, he should be fired. Anders agreed. However, in his sworn deposition, Hance claimed that the three did not concur in advance to fire Leach if he proceeded with his legal action against the university. Hance claims that he did not reply to Turner's email, explaining, "I don't know if I read the entire thing."

Others of the eleven-member Board of Regents, previously left out of the discussions between Hance, Anders, and Turner, also began to weigh in on the controversy. Nancy Neal, a board member for less than a year, emailed Turner on December 29 expressing her concerns, correspondence that Turner forwarded to Anders the next day. Neal wrote, "Any hope for outcome other than the path we are on? Doctor's letter [Phy's evaluation that James had not been harmed by this treatment] really hurts us. Said it may have helped him to do what was ordered. Where did that come from? Is there any other hope to make this right?"

Neal concluded, "I'm pleading that the course we are on wait until Monday after the game. If we owe the money, …let's not be so cheap that it isn't paid."

However it happened and whatever tipped the scales, by the morning of December 30, the decision had been made. In the halls of the Lubbock County Courthouse outside the courtroom,

Tech Counsel Campbell intercepted Liggett and advised him that if he proceeded to the scheduled hearing on the TRO, Tech would fire Leach as both coach and Tech employee. When Liggett replied that he intended to proceed, Campbell reached into his brief case and handed Liggett a letter signed by President Guy Bailey terminating Leach from his position as head coach of the Red Raiders for cause effective December 30.

Chapter 14

Aftermath: the Reactions, the Smears, the Lawsuits

The day after Mike Leach's suspension but before his firing, S. C. Gwynne wrote in *Texas Monthly,* "If Tech fires Leach over this, there will be a mushroom cloud over Lubbock that will be visible for thousands of miles and a likely revolt of Tech fans, alums, and former players." Gwynne proved to be extremely conservative in his prediction.

Windy Sitton, the first female mayor of Lubbock and a former Texas Tech University Board of Regents member, emailed Vice Chair Jerry Turner hours after the announcement of Leach's termination on December 30, 2009. She summed up the feelings of many of the Red Raider Nation when she wrote, "I want you to know that I am very upset with the end result of what happened today. How in the world can the Regents justify suspending, much less firing Mike Leach, over this issue. Maybe he made mistakes, but people have a sense of justice. This action did not rise to the level of suspension much less firing him. Why can TT not relish in success? Mike Leach is not perfect by any means, but he cares about his students, he wins games, he fills the seats, he has brought us from last to second in graduation rates. I do not understand why TT has never supported him. I guess we just want to go back to mediocrity. Jerry, I know his firing has been in the works since the Chancellor and the AD were out maneuvered by Leach. That is our problem. The problem rests with arrogance of the Chancellor and the ineptness of the AD. Everyone sees through this injustice to Mike Leach and Texas Tech. The Sitton family has given scholarships and has had multiple seats since 1976. We will not renew our options [on] our 12 seats or for that matter our PSLs for Basketball."

Sitton concluded, "This whole thing smells, and we do not

want to be a part of this blight on Texas Tech."

Stunned and outraged Tech fans and alums sought many venues in which to express their displeasure. Bill Dean, Executive Vice President and CEO of the Texas Tech Alumni Association said in an April 2011 interview, "We received close to a thousand emails when it [the firing] occurred. Not all, but most were negative. They were adamant in their disapproval. Of the thousand, about a third were not Tech grads, another third were not members of the Association, and the final third were. Many canceled their membership and contributions."

Within hours of the suspension, a Facebook group called Team Leach formed with the purpose "to show our support in a tangible way for a coach we love." Team Leach grew to more than 55,000 members in less than ten days and began work toward its stated objective, "We are in search of answers as to the truth of what happened as far as the Tech administration is concerned and determined to bring about change to ensure nothing like this happens again at Texas Tech University."

Disgruntled fans also took to the internet blogs, large and small, to express their displeasure. They wrote, "the death of football at Texas Tech," "a dark day for Tech football," "the end of donations, winning seasons, and full stadiums," "another day that will live in infamy," "it's all about the $800,000," and "shame, shame, shame." One even alluded to home town hero Buddy Holly by writing it was "the day the music and football died." Outdoor bill-boards and newspaper advertisements in Lubbock and across Texas soon sported similar messages.

Former players weighed into the fray with letters and emails supporting Leach. Eric Morris, Wes Welker, Graham Harrell and others wrote about their respect for Leach and described the negative attitude displayed by Adam James both on and off the field.

Many newspaper and blog sportswriters admitted that they were scratching their heads over Tech's dismissal of Leach. Most attempted to offer a balanced report but stated that it was difficult to defend the actions of Texas Tech. Sally Jenkins, writing in the

Washington Post a day after the firing, quipped, "You can hear the sound of a railroading in Lubbock, and it's not coming from the train station."

Jenkins continued, "Actually nothing in this case is simple. Leach is not some head-banging throwback. He's idiosyncratic and incurably outspoken, but nothing suggests he's a sadist or an idiot who would endanger a player. In fact he is one of the more well-read and thoughtful men in the game….More importantly, he's a serious, demanding educator whose team has a graduation rate of 79 percent, eighth best in the country and first in the Big 12 Conference."

Even the *National Lampoon: The Humor Magazine* got into the discussion with a lengthy, surprisingly in-depth and mostly accurate account of events. Accompanying the article was a picture of Adam James with the caption, "Tool: Every shed has one!"

The Wall Street Journal, three days after Leach's termination, reported that "three current and former members of the school's board of regents said the firing was largely the result of ill will left over from a heated contract negotiation early last year." The article quoted Jerry Turner talking about Leach's agents, "They were trying to get us to put pressure on the athletic director and force Tech to come to the terms they wanted. The way they tried dragging people into the negotiation process, we took offense to that. It's really hard to forget things like that." Other than showing insights into the seemingly unforgiving, vindictive personal nature of Turner, his statement also makes public that Leach's agents had to deal with Tech regents in addition to the university's athletic director and president.

At the Alamo Bowl, where the Tech team now coached by defensive coordinator Ruffin McNeill defeated Michigan State 41-31, airplanes circled the stadium pulling banners thanking Leach for "ten great years" and sarcastically thanking Tech officials for "an alleged investigation." In the stands students and fans held signs saying, "Headline: Craig Kills 2nd Football Program," "We didn't wanna get rid of Leach…He was put on

Craig's list," and "Every **S**issy **P**layer **N**eeds Daddy [First letters spelling out ESPN].

Sean Pendergast, echoing Gwynne's *Texas Monthly* insights, wrote in the *Houston Press* on December 31, 2009, "If you turn your attention to the west, you will see a large mushroom cloud...that's Lubbock. Specifically, the nuclear fallout is Texas Tech University, which has never been more fractured seemingly over some prima donna son of a prima donna who wound up standing in some room for a few hours."

Mike Leach made a statement shortly after his termination was announced. He thanked his supporters, outlined the accomplishment of his teams over the past decade, and assured everyone that it was now time for him to seek legal action.

The initial public and media reactions to the Leach dismissal overwhelmingly favored the coach. Virtually the only open support of Texas Tech in this affair was, not surprisingly, from ESPN—Craig James' employer. The triad of James/ESPN, Spaeth Communications, and Texas Tech itself were quickly on the offensive to apparently spin the story away from the facts and to smear the reputation of Mike Leach.

Once Craig James accomplished his objective of getting Leach terminated, he seemingly changed his position and his stories. He now claimed, despite the emails and witness statements that proved otherwise, that he was surprised by the firing of Leach and that all he ever wanted was to look out for the health of his son and to receive an apology from the coach. James also began referring to his dispute with Leach as "a spiritual war," leaving the listener or reader to determine just what he meant by that phrase. Meanwhile, James and his employer ESPN seemed to be doing everything possible—spiritual or not—to ruin Leach's reputation as a coach and as an individual.

In an ESPN televised interview a day after Leach's suspension and a day before his termination, James said, "I'm a dad. Everybody knows me as an ESPN guy and a football guy, but I'm a dad. When my wife and I heard about it the first time, we had no idea how to respond. The second time it came to us, we really wanted to help protect Adam from further things that could go against him. This is not common sense, the tactics and tools and the methods he was placed under following a doctor's diagnosis of a concussion." Apparently James was already getting his money's worth from Spaeth Communications as it was they who apparently prepared much of this statement.

ESPN usually does it best to present both sides of issues and to remain neutral. It appears that the network, however, did not follow this standard in the James case and the resulting coverage of Leach's termination. But to give credit where credit is due, it must be noted the organization at least stood by its long-term employee—something Texas Tech evidently did not do for their coach of ten years.

The sports network did replace James with Bob Davie as analyst for the upcoming Alamo Bowl but left Craig's long-term partner Mike Patrick as the game's play-by-play announcer. During the January 2 Alamo Bowl, with its television of audience of eight million, the commentators—Patrick, Davie, and the ESPN studio—spent 28 total minutes of the four-hour game, including commercial breaks, commenting on Leach's termination. No one offered any defense of the coach.

In fact, the Alamo Bowl coverage was so blatantly pro-James, anti-Leach that ESPN Ombudsman Don Ohlmeyer, a longtime NBC and ABC executive who had earned 16 Emmys including a Lifetime Achievement Award, condemned the display. He wrote in an article published by ESPN on January 21, 2010, "The announcers talked off-game over plays, replays, the referees' penalty calls and even each other. They had to interrupt what amounted to a sports radio talk show about Leach to pick up, in progress, several big plays, including a touchdown. They misidentified players and were late recognizing a fake field goal attempt. At one time, they went nine plays without verbalizing down and distance."

One example Ohlmeyer noted was early in the game when the cameras panned to the sidelines and Patrick pointed and said, "There is Adam James, who is the young man who was actually punished for having a concussion."

In his article, Ohlmeyer described the halftime report in which Davie aired part of a New Year's Eve interview with Leach in which the coach "suggested James would use his position at ESPN as an analyst to leverage playing time for his son." In a follow up clip, James was shown responding, "It is absurd." In yet another instance the ombudsman pointed out that Davie referred to Craig James as "courageous."

Ohlmeyer concluded, "Taking a captive audience and using it as prop to further interests put that good will at risk—and ESPN needs to remember there's not an endless supply."

Whatever the motivation of ESPN and its announcers, the Alamo Bowl was a ratings success. It drew a 5.6 rating, the most watched bowl game in ESPN history—in all likelihood because of the Mike Leach termination.

Despite the network ombudsman's position that ESPN was in danger of harming its own reputation with the kind of coverage it provided for the Alamo Bowl, James continued to use the network to make his case. Meanwhile, Spaeth Communications associates were working just as hard behind the scenes. In addition to providing advice and written statements for the James family, the public relations company evidently began working directly with Texas Tech and ESPN to spin the story.

Spaeth Communications appears to have focused primarily on getting the so called "electrical closet" video taken by Adam James on as many venues as possible, in spreading negative comments about Leach, and in adapting and adjusting the Tech side of the controversy when necessary. Merrie Spaeth's primary operatives in this campaign were her Executive Vice President Rebecca Shaw and independent journalist Brooke Robbins.

Already employed by James since at least December 19, Spaeth was ready to release information and statements to ESPN and other outlets as soon as Leach's suspension was announced on December 28. Stories about Adam James being locked in an "electrical closet" dominated the airways. Late that evening, VP Rebecca Shaw emailed Craig James, "Let's take a look at the coverage the first thing in the morning and make a decision then if we want to forward the players' names and numbers exclusive to Joe [Shad at ESPN], whether we want to include the AP reporter, or if we want to hold off for a day to see if the university makes a statement. I'll be up early checking the coverage. Merrie's good with the statement that I drafted for you for ESPN. Would you like it circulated…?"

Not all of Spaeth's staff were quite so enthusiastic. On the morning of December 29, a firm employee emailed Shaw, "After an initial burst of postings by Leach haters, we're getting killed on the blogs." The staffer then summarized saying that some blog entries called Craig James a prima donna, others blamed the contentious contract negotiations, and some suggested political foul play. He also wrote, "I am not so young that I don't remember James bringing down SMU 25 years ago."

Early in the afternoon of December 29, journalist Brooke Robbins emailed Merrie Spaeth, discussing the possible problems of Craig James' involvement in the SMU "Death Penalty" and saying, "Let's get focus off James as a part of that old mess."

Spaeth responded an hour later, "Brooke of course, if you felt you could log on with a pseudoname [sic] onto the blogs and share those thoughts, it would be wonderful…"

Early on December 30, Spaeth again emailed Robbins after apparently receiving instructions from Craig James, "Brooke—we have the go ahead. I envision this as the simplest of interview(s) with you and doctors, etc., posted on YouTube. We need to get something up today, I envision all of these would go something like this: 'I'm Brooke Robbins, an independent journalist. We've all heard the news about Texas Tech Coach Mike Leach and the player who had a concussion. The Coach is saying it was 'only' a 'mild' concussion. Over the past year or so, there have been a high number of high profile stories about players with concussions. We're going to ask some leading doctors, sports medicine experts and trainers—what's the proper treatment for a concussion? Can you 'fake' a concussion, the way coach Leach charges, just how serious is a concussion? If you have a child who plays football, or you're just a concerned parent or citizen, let's look into this together...'"

All of this took place before the termination of Leach. Once he was officially fired, Spaeth Communications appeared to ratchet up their smear campaign with Craig James continuing to pay their bills.

Although placing the concussion video on YouTube had Spaeth's approval, Spaeth did not do the actual dirty work; Brooke Robbins took care of that task on the evening of December 30. The next morning, VP Shaw emailed Robbins about the posting of the video with her interviews, stating, "Nice job. This has great information in it." Shaw then expressed her concern about the few "hits'" the video was receiving.

Robbins responded in the early afternoon of the 31st (capitalizations hers), "When I created the YouTube account, I put in the following key words: "concussion, James, Leach, Coach Leach, Mike Leach, Adam James, Craig James, sports concussions, Texas Tech sports...And a few more. When people google any of the words...Our you tube [sic] will EVENTUALLY come up. It takes a while for search engines to find these new things."

She continued, "What could expedite the process if a few of YOU have the time and desire to go onto some of the blogs and say things like...'Hey I came across this new you tube [sic]...Then paste in the link... That really has great info on concussions...' That's one grass roots way of generating hits...We can also keep hitting it ourselves."

The afternoon of December 31, Robbins uploaded the "electrical closet" video onto YouTube. The next morning she emailed Shaw saying it had been up for 12 hours and was getting a decent number of hits "for a holiday weekend."

By the afternoon of January 1, 2010, the electrical closet video had received 120,000 hits on YouTube. Then Spaeth Communications linked it to the concussion interviews Robbins had conducted for Spaeth. This was posted as Spaethcomm8181. Soon the videos were appearing in an almost constant loop on

ESPN as well as other media outlets.

Merrie Spaeth, however, was not happy with this identification tag, writing in an email, "Did no one think that this connects our name with this?"

Spaeth may not have been pleased that her company's name and actions were publicly connected to the concussion interviews, but that did not slow her public relations efforts on the part of her employer Craig James. In fact, she expanded her efforts to assist and advise Texas Tech officials on how to spin the story.

On the evening of January 1 [one has to wonder if holiday or overtime rates were being charged], Spaeth emailed Sally Post, the director of Communications and Broadcast Media for Texas Tech. In reference to the initial statements given by Dr. Michael Phy and Head Trainer Steve Pincock, Spaeth wrote, "Sally—I assume you and the Chancellor have seen these. We will not make any comment until we talk to you and let me know what the University had done.

"--The Doctor: other than the 'mild-concussion (There is no such thing.) it's not really in dispute. The issue isn't whether the other treatment harmed Adam…But he needs to confirm the diagnosis, recant 'mild' and talk about the need for rest, etc.

"--The Trainer: this is rather dramatically different account than Adam's and from what we understand he provided to the university. How to handle?"

Within an hour Post answered with Steve Pincock's statement and the message, "Here's what the trainer told Charlotte. It is NOT signed."

Just how much additional assistance Spaeth rendered to Post and Texas Tech is not public; however, the university was deeply involved in damage and spin control on its own. In its statement following the Leach termination, the officials stated, "It is our number one priority to protect the welfare of our students and the reputation of Texas Tech University." (Appendix C)

In order to protect the University's reputation, the administration—on the apparent advice from and with the assistance of Spaeth—was already taking measures to get Phy and Pincock to provide new, somewhat different statements, from the ones they gave to their own coaching staff. Chancellor Hance, a former lobbyist himself and a man experienced in manipulating the media, made statements saying that only Leach was responsible for his firing and that anyone who sues his boss should expect to get fired. At the same time, he and members of the Board of Regents—in an apparent effort to distance themselves from their own direct involvement—took every opportunity to praise President Bailey and AD Myers for their termination action.

Jim Sowell, the Tech mega-donor who had held so much animosity toward Leach since the contract negotiations, was not part of the email about Leach's ultimate termination, yet he emailed a statement to Pete Christy, the sports director at KCBD-TV in Lubbock, stating, "Any suggestion that there was a premeditated plan a year ago to fire him after he signed his new contract is nonsense."

As if the "electrical closet" video were not damning enough, just before depositions were to begin in the spring of 2010, suddenly there appeared other video of Mike Leach. This time it was the uncut, "for internal use only" clips of Leach in front of his players at team meetings. In March 2010, Chip Brown of orangebloods. com released videos of Leach in obscenity-laced locker room rants to his team after victories over Kansas and Baylor the previous year. More similar videos—shot with the understanding between Leach and Tech that they would not be released to the public except in small, heavily edited clips at booster clubs and similar settings—surfaced. It is not always possible to connect all the dots in a scattered story, but sometimes the dots are just to egregious to ignore—connecting line or not.

This agreement about the videoed material had been honored until the day before Chancellor Hance's sworn deposition. That is when Russell Thomasson, the special assistant and counsel to the Chancellor, took possession of the videos. Almost immediately after the transfer, blogger Brown, under the Texas Open Records Act, was able to obtain the videos, which he then posted on his web site, YouTube, and other outlets. Just how Brown knew to request the videos remains a mystery. What is a matter of record is that Brown is an SMU graduate and a friend of Craig James. Multiple phone calls and emails to Brown for an explanation have gone unanswered.

One other interesting dot on the record to which there are no published lines is the reversal of position by the former mayor who seems to have had a complete change of heart. Once the litigation began, Windy Sitton, still quite active in the Lubbock business and social scene, submitted an affidavit concerning her email of December 30. In her statement on May 6, 2010, Sitton explained, "That email was sent in haste and I very much regret sending it."

Sitton explained that her initial reactions were based on conversations with Leach and she had now changed her mind after getting additional information. She concluded, "Again, I regret the remarks that I made in my email about Mr. Hance and Mr. Myers, as I know them to be loyal and steadfast supporters and alumni of Texas Tech University. I have renewed my season tickets to Texas Tech Football and remain, as I hope all Tech alumni do, a loyal supporter of Texas Tech and Texas Tech Football." Efforts by Tech lawyers to exclude the original Sitton letter from further litigation were refused by the court. It is notable that while Sitton twice stated that she "regrets" the content of her email, at no point does she recant her original statement.

Within a few days following his termination, Mike Leach, through the concentrated smear and spin campaign by the triad, had mostly been judged in the court of public opinion. Now it was time for Leach to enter the real courts in pursuit of the truth and in an effort to restore his reputation.

On January 12, 2010, Leach's attorney's filed action against Texas Tech University in the 99th Judicial District Court in Lubbock. The suit accuses Tech of breach of contract because Leach was suspended without due process in that he was not given 10 days, as outlined in his contract, to present an explanation or cure to the allegations. It also includes charges of slander, libel, fraud, and negligent misrepresentation. Finally, it charges Tech with violating the Texas Whistleblower Act for firing an employee who in good faith reports a violation of law. Over the next weeks Leach's lawsuit expanded to include—along with Tech—Kent Hance, Jerry Turner, Larry Anders, Craig James, Guy Bailey, Gerald Myers, and Charlotte Bingham.

On November 24, 2010, Leach filed a separate lawsuit against ESPN and Spaeth Communications. The petition states, "This case concerns the willful and negligent defamation of Plaintiff Mike Leach by Defendant ESPN, the world's most prominent sports network. ESPN published and failed to retract false and damaging statements based on misinformation it obtained in large part from Craig James, an ESPN announcer, who ESPN knew to be hostile to Leach. Craig James' son, Adam James, had made accusations of mistreatment that underlay the controversy. This suit also concerns the false, misleading, and defamatory campaign against Leach by Spaeth Communications, a public relations firm hired by Craig James for the purpose of creating public opinion hostile to Leach."

Chapter 15

Life Goes On: Where They Are Today

As of this writing in the early fall of 2011, the Mike Leach/ Texas Tech story remains in the national sports news. Leach's biography, *Swing Your Sword*, refocused attention on the simmering controversy with its release in July of this year. All of the participants remain affected by the controversy—some more than others. Life goes on for all, but there is little doubt that sometime in their future, all of the players in this drama will again be tied to this event at Texas Tech University during the closing days of 2009—whether in a news article, bio, or obituary. The following provides an update on the major participants and actions.

Kent Hance remains the Chancellor of the Texas Tech University System. On May 1, 2011, Tech announced that Hance had donated 60 percent of the funding for a $3 million non-denominational chapel to be built on campus. The facility will be named the "Kent R. Hance Chapel," in accordance with a university policy (where more than 50 percent of a building's cost is covered by a donor, the building is to be named for the principal contributor).

Critics point to the irony of the chapel's name, not only because of the seemingly dubious actions of its major benefactor in the Leach controversy but also because part of Hance's wealth is derived from his ownership of a portion of Waste Control Specialists, a company that many believe is polluting the largest aquifer in the United States and the source of much of the ground water for Lubbock and Texas Tech.

Guy Bailey remains the president of Texas Tech University. Jerry Turner and Larry Anders still sit on the Tech Board of Regents. Turner's term expires in 2013, Anders' in 2017. On February 24, 2011, Turner was elected Chairman of the Board of

Regents. Charlotte Bingham and Grace Hernandez continue to be employed by the university.

Gerald Myers, still holding the record for the second-best basketball free throw record in Tech history, retired as University Athletic Director on May 31, 2011. Kirby Hocutt—a native Texan, a former linebacker for Kansas State, and the Athletic Director at the University of Miami—replaced Myers. In an article by Mike Jones in the May 29, 2011, edition of the *Fort Worth Star-Telegram,* President Guy Bailey is quoted as saying, "I thought this guy would fit right into West Texas. Everything I've seen verifies that." Chancellor Hance also played a role in lobbying Hocutt to return to his home state.

Texas Tech football and other sports programs have, of course, continued. On January 9, 2010, less than two weeks after terminating Leach, Tech hired former Auburn University coach Tommy Tuberville as his replacement. The Red Raiders went 8-5 in Tuberville's first season as head coach, but three of the losses were to Texas, Oklahoma, and Texas A&M—the first time that had occurred since 2001. Tuberville's defense ranked number 114 in the country and his Red Raiders outscored their opponents 430-402 opposed to 481-292 the previous season. Ticket sales were reported to be off by 35 percent. It should be noted that this was a team that Leach had expected to win the conference—one of the reasons he suggested an exit strategy that would give him one more season in Lubbock.

A year after hiring him, Tech raised Tuberville's salary by a half million dollars a year, increasing his pay to $2 million annually despite several professors' protesting the raise amid cut backs in the university's budget. In March 2011, Brooks Melchior in his sportsbybrooks.com blog wrote, "Tuberville is absolutely miserable at Texas Tech….One of his complaints is ADs Myers/Hocutt are powerless to keep admins and boosters in check." Tuberville denied the story.

Steve Pincock, the head trainer under Leach, was demoted to assistant athletic trainer. Tuberville hired his former head trainer at Auburn, Arnold Gamber, to come to Tech. At the time Gamber was being sued by former Auburn player Chaz Ramsey for mishandling the back injury that ended Ramsey's football career. Ironically, Texas Tech, who had fired Leach for allegedly abusing a player, seemed to embrace the hire.

Shortly after the termination of Mike Leach, Tech officials informed Patty Ross that the university was going in "a different direction" and dismissed her. After 35 years working for Tech and as the senior administrative assistant to six head football coaches she had been let go with no further explanation. Ross currently is employed by a Lubbock law firm.

Texas Tech remains a university of significance and a central part of Lubbock. However, the road for its sports programs has not been smooth or un-blighted, as controversy did not depart the university with Leach. While it had terminated their most successful football coach ever for alleged abuses, the system continued to tolerate real character flaws with the new and remaining staff.

Tuberville's defensive coordinator James Willis resigned after being accused of domestic violence against his wife in December 2010. Willis later pled guilty to the charge.

Character issues have also surfaced in regard to Tuberville himself and his association with Auburn and its treatment of players. In March 2011, four of his former players at Auburn revealed to HBO's *RealSports* that they had received cash payments while being recruited by or playing for the Tigers.

When Tech hired Billy Gillispie as basketball coach in March 2011, he brought with him to Lubbock three drinking and driving arrests on his record. He had, while coaching at Kentucky, allegedly forced a player to spend half time in a locker room toilet stall and then made him ride home from the game in the equipment truck rather than on the team bus.

Hiring basketball coaches with baggage was nothing new for Texas Tech. When Bobby Knight arrived in Lubbock in 2001, he had been fired from Indiana for physically abusing his players. He also had been convicted in absentia in Puerto Rico for allegedly assaulting a police officer. Knight had once thrown a chair across the basketball court to protest a referee's call, and he had been accused of making sexist statements.

Despite his past and his temperament, Knight was extremely popular with Athletic Director Myers and some of the regents. He did not get along so well with Chancellor David R. Smith. In 2004, at a Lubbock grocery store, Knight felt patronized by Smith and verbally attacked him, following him out into the parking lot with additional insults. Myers and board members came to Knight's defense. Eventually Myers signed a slap-on-the-wrist letter to Knight that included a three-day suspension.

Knight remained at Tech until his retirement in 2008—at which point he took a job as a commentator for ESPN. His son Pat was named his successor at Tech until being replaced by Gillespie.

Not only have personnel problems presented the university with challenges, but also adequate fundraising levels have been difficult to maintain, especially with recent state budget revenue cuts. In June 2011, the university announced a 5.9 percent increase, or about $500 per student per year, in tuition beginning with the fall semester. On August 5, 2011, Tech's Board of Regents announced that the 2012 system wide budget would increase by less than one percent—the smallest in 20 years and requiring a cut of 600 jobs. That is not to say, however, that money would not be available for "pet projects." The regents approved a new indoor soccer field, to be named in honor of former athletic director Gerald Myers, at the cost of $900,000.

The regent's announcement continued with a claim that they planned to fundraise $1 billion. The results of this campaign may be difficult to verify. On October 23, 2010 the *Lubbock Avalanche-Journal* ran a story by Matthew McGowan stating that on-air claims by ESPN that Tuberville had a financial impact of $25 million were incorrect—only $1.25 million in donations could be attributed to the new coach. Tech denied providing the larger figure to ESPN; the sports network said they could not say where they got their incorrect information.

All of this is further indicative that Texas Tech may be on shaky financial footing. In 2006, the University's annual debt service, the cash required to cover the repayment of a debt's interest and principal, was $5,739,277. By 2009 the number had risen to $16,897,797.

Tech has also evidently encountered difficulties in meeting the criteria by which an emerging research university qualifies for funding from the National Research University Fund (NRUF). Part of the requirement is to show awards and distinctions earned by the faculty as verified by the Texas Higher Education Coordinating Board (THECB).

In one case, Tech claimed Dr. Katharine Hayhoe to be a Nobel Laureate when, in fact, she was only one of a group of more than a thousand scientists recognized as a group for the award. In their investigation, the THECB discovered on Tech's own website a quote from Dr. Hayhoe noting that she did not claim to be a Nobel Laureate. Additionally, the THECB discovered that Tech professors Lara Crowly and Jacqueline Kolosoz-Wenthe were not full-time National Endowment for the Humanities fellows as the University claimed. Other discrepancies indicated misreporting years of awards to increase annual totals.

Another error discovered by THECB was in the way Tech allegedly attempted to secure matching funds from the Texas Research Incentive Program (TRIP). Their investigation showed that about a quarter of a million dollars of donations for which the university was requesting matching funds did not qualify under their rather straight forward regulations. In order to qualify for further NRUF funding, Tech has also been found to be using a creative, regulation-violating method to calculate the average ACT and SAT averages of its incoming freshmen.

In addition, apparently Tech has not provided reported expenditures of research funds—instead offering its strategic proposal for research and intended fund dispersal goals. In a manner very similar to its handling of the termination of Mike Leach, Texas Tech is extremely closed-handed in providing any information on these matters. What is included here was not freely provided by the university but rather came through Public

Information Act and Open Records requests.

Adam James remained on the Tech football team for the 2010 season. Based on his playing time during that period, Tuberville evidently was no more impressed with the receiver than Leach had been. James appeared in nine games and caught only two passes, 13 fewer than in 2008 and 15 fewer than in 2009, for 26 total yards. He has one year of eligibility remaining and is on the roster for the 2011 season.

The younger James apparently continues to consider himself entitled, exempt from rules and regulations, and unconcerned with monetary issues. In May 2011, Texas Tech parking officials conducted their annual sweep of the campus for abandoned or illegally parked bicycles and other two-wheelers. Among the confiscations was a motorized scooter parked illegally and abandoned—registered in the name of Adam James.

Craig James is still employed by ESPN. He is also getting involved in Texas politics. He has since expressed interests in running for the open Texas U.S. Senate seat in 2012, but a poll by Lincoln Park Strategies of Washington, D.C., of voters from Lubbock, Amarillo, and Midland/Odessa shows James achieving a remarkable zero (0) percent of the votes in a ten person field. The poll noted that James had only a 8 percent positive opinion rating.

Despite these numbers, James is still exploring the possibilities of placing his hat back in the ring. In June 2011 James announced his founding of "Texans for a Better America," which is "about reconnecting people with the values, ideas, and founding principles that have not only made Texas the envy of our nation, but would transform our country." The video released with the announcement proclaims, "Craig James is a living example of the importance of economic freedom and America's entrepreneurial spirit." The organization's web site prominently solicits contributions.

On August 1, 2011, awfulannouncing.com selected James as the "Awful Announcer of the Year." James defeated 32 other major sports announcers for the title that drew more than 50,000 votes in the semi-final and finals alone. Cam Martin, writing on the same date in mediabistro.com explained the reasons behind the announcer's "victory," said, "Simply, Craig James took part in a false character assassination using his position in the college football media on the 'leader' [ESPN] to do nothing more than carry out his petty, childish, pathetic personal agenda."

Other sports reporters have also expressed their opinions about Craig James. SI.com published the results of a roundtable discussion moderated by Richard Deitsch on August 26, 2011. Deitsch asked, "Which college football announcer/s are the least appealing for you and why?"

Sports Illustrated reporter Andy Staples answered, "Craig James, because he adds very little to the broadcast, and ESPN has sacrificed much of its journalistic integrity to protect him in the wake of his campaign to get Mike Leach fired at Texas Tech. If ESPN replaced James with any random ex-jock, viewers wouldn't complain a bit. Yet for some reason, the network had bent over backward to protect James. It makes no sense."

To the same question, sports reporter George Schroeder responded, "Other than Craig James? Even aside from the helicopter-dad/Mike Leach/Texas Tech stuff, I'm not a big fan."

Deitsch concluded this part of the discussion saying, "That Craig James gets such prominent assignments remains a mystery on the D. B. Cooper scale. He is unpopular by any fan metric you chose, including performance and likeability. The fact that former Texas Tech coach Mike Leach is suing James merely adds noise here. ESPN management says it values James for his relationships with coaches but what that ultimately leads to for viewers is little more than backslapping commentary. The network deserves to get crushed for keeping him on the air."

Deitsch continued the roundtable discussion asking, "Do you trust Craig James when it comes to reporting on the Big 12?"

College football writer Steward Mandel responded, "I wouldn't trust Craig James to report on sixth-grade volleyball. It's been established, via documented emails, that he not only encouraged a sitting Big 12 football coach's dismissal but hired a PR firm to intentionally manipulate coverage. And yet he's still walking into Big 12 coaches' offices every week to break down tape. Now he's running partisan political ads, which you would think would be a no-no for a television analyst."

To the same question, Staples answered, "No. But I don't trust him when it comes to reporting on anything."

Schroeder added, "Does he report? I'm not sure how ESPN justifies keeping him around."

ESPN has kept a low profile in the Leach/Tech affairs since the initial burst of controversy. They have made no official comments on Leach's lawsuit and Spaeth communications other than to say it is "without merit" and that they will defend themselves "vigorously." The only recent significant action on the subject by the sports network took place after the release of Leach's biography *Swing Your Sword*. On July 14, 2011, ESPN banned Bruce Feldman, an ESPN reporter and Leach editor/co-author, from writing for any of the network's entities. They also prohibited him from appearing on any ESPN platform, stopped his twitter account, and forbade his participation in any promotion of Leach's book. From all accounts, Feldman had received permission from ESPN to assist in the book prior to his assisting Leach.

Almost immediately after the ESPN announcement, Feldman's fellow journalists and friends created a twitter hashtag and a Facebook page supporting him. Comments critical of the sports network's decision, as well as positive comments about Leach and his book, soon filled the sites. Even Craig James, in an apparent effort to share no responsibility in the decision of his employer, tweeted, "Respected colleague & friend of Feldman since early 90s. Surprised! Saw this in news like y'all."

Less than 24 hours after their suspension announcement, ESPN recognized the overwhelming support for Feldman and their public relations blunder. In a "we said" but "we did not say" explanation, network spokesperson Josh Krulewitz announced in a July 15 email, "There was never any suspension or any other form of disciplinary action. We took the time to review his upcoming work assignments in light of the book to which he contributed and will manage any conflicts or other issues as needed. Bruce has resumed his assignments." Meanwhile, all this news coverage pushed Leach's book up in sales and in the rankings on the *Publishers Weekly* and *New York Time Book Review* best seller lists. Leach's book signings in Lubbock, Houston, Dallas, and Oklahoma City set attendance and sales records.

Requests to ESPN for further comment or explanation produced a one-sentence reply from the network spokesman. On July 29, 2011, Krulewitz emailed, "We have no additional comment beyond what we said publicly."

While ESPN would make no comment to this author, the network did make a loud statement to Bruce Feldman. In an interview on September 6, 2011, Feldman elaborated on his departure from ESPN. He explained that during the time of the controversy over his participation in the Leach book, he completed his seventeenth year working for the sports network—one of its first hires when it was established. With his contract nearing its end, he had been promised a new three-year agreement with a substantial raise in salary. At the end of August, however, ESPN offered him only a one-year deal without a raise, differences they based on what they stated was loss of "creditability."

Feldman apparently understood that ESPN wanted him to quit. He did so and quickly accepted an offer from CBS Sports— one of five employment opportunities open to him. As for the creditably issue, he told his old bosses, "Wait a minute, you are bringing up my creditability and my future with the company and you guys still put Craig James on the air?"

Feldman added that he must be able to trust people he works for, and he had lost that trust with ESPN. He also stated that all he wanted was to get back to reporting on sports, back to being the interviewer rather than the interviewee. When asked directly about his opinion of Craig James, all Feldman would say was that if the sports announcer was running for a public office, he would not vote for him.

Spaeth Communications continues its operations in Dallas.

On December 21, 2010, in response to the lawsuit filed by Leach, the public relations firm's insurance company also filed a suit seeking permission to drop coverage of the communications company. Hartford Lloyds Insurance Company claims that Spaeth's business liability coverage does not cover the accusations as outlined in Leach's suit.

In response to Leach's suit, Spaeth Communications cites its rights to free speech under the First Amendment and claims that Leach cannot prove he was damaged by any of the remarks provided by Spaeth to ESPN and Craig James. Spaeth further claims that Leach has no case because the statements made about him are essentially true—and even if they were not true, they were not said with any malice.

Spaeth Communications and Craig James are represented in the lawsuits brought by Leach by Scott McLaughlin of Jackson Walker, L.L.P., in Houston, Texas. In an email on August 2, 2011, McLaughlin stated in part, "I believe that Texas Tech's evidence demonstrates that Mike Leach could have easily saved his job, but rejected that opportunity in favor of maintaining the position that it was acceptable to confine a consussed [sic] player to a shed, and then a pitch black (literally) room, both times for extended periods of time."

In the same communiqué, McLaughlin indicated that only one side of this story is currently "in the record and the other side of the story not yet available," an odd positioning for the public relations' company representative given that Spaeth Communications was only too eager to present all the "facts" and stories it could manufacture when Leach was the target.

Team Leach remains an active group of the coach's supporters. One of the team's current administrators, J. R. Ghaddar of Austin, reported in a June 2011 interview that the Team has maintained a membership of 50,000-55,000 members of all ages, backgrounds and origins. Their common bond remains a support of Leach and a desire that the truth behind his termination be revealed. Ghaddar, a self- described "huge fan of college football," is a good example of the team's diverse membership. He is an alumnus of the University of Texas and the University of Southern California who did not attend Texas Tech.

Leach remains in contact with many of his Tech fans. When Team Leach member Keri Kuczek of Killeen was seriously injured in an automobile accident in October 2010, Leach frequently called her and her family during her convalescence. Kuczek joined Leach at his Dallas book signing on July 26, 2011. Carol Cavazos of CBSDFW.com reported, "While some might think of Mike Leach as an 'Old Salt,' his heart is in the right place. Fans like Keri Kuczek already know that."

Leach's lawsuits continue to make their way through the court systems moving at a slow pace. Texas Tech continues to defend itself with the claim that the university acted properly in terminating Leach because of his improper treatment of an injured athlete and his insubordination. The university further claims sovereign immunity, which, according to Texas law, means that a state agency or entity cannot be sued without its permission. Leach's lawyers claim that the egregious actions on the part of the university vacates its sovereign immunity rights. Some legal scholars take the position that if Tech has sovereign immunity in this case, then the university does not have to adhere to any contract it signs, or for that matter, does not need to sign any contracts at all.

Initial court decisions ruled that Tech officials—including Hance, Bailey, Myers, Turner, Anders, and Bingham—could not be included in the suit. On January 21, 2011, the 7th Court of Appeals upheld Tech's sovereign immunity claim but allowed Leach to continue his suit to try to show the university's reasons for firing him were wrong. It added, however, that no monetary damages would be awarded regardless of outcome.

Interestingly, the 7th Court of Appeals is composed entirely of Texas Tech graduates. Of the four members, two earned both their undergraduate and law degrees from the university. One received his BA at Tech while the fourth graduated from its law school.

Leach approached the Texas Legislature to request that body

grant permission to waive sovereign immunity. The bill never came before the legislature, dying on the calendar.

The decision by 7th Court of Appeals allowed the suit against Tech and Craig James to return to the jurisdiction of the 99th District Court. If this court determines Tech violated the coach's right to legal remedy when they terminated him, it will help clear Leach's name. Sometime in the fall of 2011, the Texas Supreme Court is expected to decide whether Leach can sue Tech for monetary damages.

Leach's suit against Spaeth Communications and ESPN is in a Lubbock State District Court and it, too, is stayed while awaiting the decision of the Texas Supreme Court. It is anticipated that all the cases will be combined if and when they go to a jury trial.

Meanwhile, Tech has failed to pay Leach even more than the $800,000 completion bonus. A *Dallas Morning News* article on June 2, 2010 by Dwain Price reported that the university still owed Leach $1.7 million for the 2009 season. This included $1.6 million in guaranteed outside athletic-related personal income and $25,000 bonuses each for Tech playing in a bowl game, finishing number 21 in the AP Poll, for winning five Big 12 games, and for maintaining a graduation rate of more than 65 percent. According to Leach's contract, he was supposed to receive these revenues no later than the previous February 15.

A subsequent Open Records Request by the *Fort Worth Star-Telegram* resulted in a Tech claim that they had paid the $100,000 in bonuses but that it did not owe the $1.6 million because Leach was not entitled to the money because he had been fired.

In an article in the June 1, 2011 edition of the *Washington Post*, Rich Maese wrote about Leach's post-termination life, "There are palm trees in purgatory." On July 12, SI.com proclaimed, "the coach in exile waits in paradise." Both headlines refer to the fact that Mike Leach and his family now live in Key West, Florida while waiting for the outcome of his court cases and for the next job offer to appear. He was a strong candidate for the Maryland job in early 2011 and his name surfaces with each opening for a coach in a major program.

Leach admits that the lawsuits limit his marketability. That and the fact that some universities are put off by Leach's supposed reputation of allegedly abusing players. Some schools are also leery that the powerful ESPN might block their national exposure on the network's game matchups or limit its coverage on *Sports Center* and other shows.

Meanwhile, Leach enjoys the beach and continues his quest for knowledge on a variety of subjects—both common and esoteric. He also remains actively employed in football, if not on the field itself then on the sidelines. During the 2010 season, Leach worked as an analyst for CBS Sports; he now has a daily radio show with co-host Jack Arute on Sirius/XM radio. He holds coaching seminars, consults, and makes guest speaker appearances. Recently, despite a previous disdain for social media, Leach launched his own Twitter site. He also has found time for a visit to Europe before returning to the United States to do a tour promoting his biography.

The support for Mike Leach by the Red Raider Nation has not waivered with the passage of time. In a survey conducted on September 2-3, 2011 and released by NASICA of Irving, Texas, on September 21, more than 82% of students and alumni surveyed expressed a favorable opinion of Coach Leach. The survey showed that 78% of all Tech students and alumni polled stated that they believed Leach should not have been fired while 67.5% felt that Chancellor Kent Hance had badly mishandled the situation. Craig James rated a 72% unfavorable opinion in the poll.

Major print and electronic media continue to seek Leach's opinions and input. Fellow coaches and former players maintain contact. On June 13, 2011, while awaiting the end of the NFL lockout so he could rejoin the San Francisco Forty-Niners, Michael Crabtree spoke for many of Leach's former players when he said, "Mike Leach always wanted to make something happen. He never took the game too seriously; he made it fun for us. Mike Leach is the best coach I ever had."

Afterword

The termination of Mike Leach created a vast, often hostile divide between proponents of the university and supporters of the coach. Few who heard the story stayed on the sidelines. The most prolific communicators on the subject of the termination, though not quoted in this work, are the anonymous posters on various internet sites who use identifications that are non-attributable. These posting are usually angry, vile, crude—if not profane—and often inaccurate. These writers contribute little or nothing to the overall discussion or understanding of the controversy. Their writings are mostly the childish rants of teenagers—no matter what their age—still living in their parents' basement.

I made every effort to gather both sides of this story from the actual participants, witnesses, and media observers. Some sources were remarkably open, others not so revealing. Many refused comment. Overall the pro-Leach factions were much better at returning telephone calls and emails, willing to answer questions and share files and records. Few Texas Tech officials and university supporters did likewise. Their strategy seems to be to "keep quiet; ignore the facts; and delay, delay, delay any actions as long as possible." Those who did respond seemed to be honestly concerned about their school's reputation and future rather than about the impact or possible consequences to themselves.

Perhaps the most interesting group of participants that I attempted to interview were Lubbock media representatives. For a group who depend on sources returning their phone calls, some of these journalists went to great lengths not only not to answer their phones—let alone give up information— but also to avoid all contact that might put them on the line. A few willingly answered questions, and those answers appear as quotes in this book; some others provided insights but asked that the information be used only as background. Others said that if they talked to me, Tech would no longer talk to them, and then they would be out of work. One reporter responded to my email, stating, "I spoke to my bosses and they feel I shouldn't take part since I need to be an unbiased journalist and that my opinions may be taken as the station's. They said with possible false perceptions, not to partake."

Not all the Leach supporters stepped forward either. Some ignored requests for comments; others seemed not to be sufficiently committed to attach their name to their beliefs. In pursuit of one of Leach's former players, now playing in the NFL, I talked with his team's office who said they could not help contact him because of the lockout. I finally tracked down his mother who, in the course of five phone calls, promised she would pass along my message for her son to give me a call. He never did.

I also cross-checked the validity of comments and quotes everywhere I could. Sometimes I found honest mistakes; sometimes I found changed stories; sometimes it was impossible to tell the difference. In one case, a quote attributed to Butch Ford, the Celina High School football coach of Adam James, received much internet coverage. The article quoted Ford as talking about how Craig James constantly interfered and how happy he was when Adam graduated. In response to my questions by telephone on June 23, 2011, Ford denied ever making the statements and said that neither Adam James nor his father had ever been a problem to his program.

Efforts to talk with Texas Tech officials, including the Chancellor and members of the Board of Regents, began in April 2011 and continued until the completion of the draft manuscript in late August 2011. My representative in Lubbock and Dallas, Michael Ogulnick, diligently pursued interviews and solicited comments across the campus. He contacted Chris Cook, the Managing Director of the university's Office of Communications and Marketing to tell him about my efforts to collect facts from both sides of the controversy. On May 20, 2011, Cook emailed,

"Thank you, Michael, for the information. We are going to decline the invitation, however."

Despite Tech's initial refusal to participate in this book, efforts continued throughout its preparation to secure their viewpoints. Finally, in late August a dialogue began via email between the author and Chris Cook. Finally, albeit more than a week later than promised, Cook provided responses to questions. Few, if any, of these replies offered any new information not already included in public interviews or in depositions but, in fairness, they are repeated within the appropriate chapters.

Mike Leach took no direct role in this book but did respond to my communications. On July 22, 2011, he wrote, "My candid, complete, and honest evaluations and comments are contained in my deposition of March 12, 2010 and in my book *Swing Your Sword*. You are welcome to refer to them as sources."

Although all these interviews—and refusals to talk, for that matter—were helpful, the major content of this book comes from the thousands of pages in the hundreds of documents related to this controversy. Much of it is from sworn testimony from court records.

Anyone who is upset or angered by their words in this book as cited should remember the writings of Aeschylus, a 5th Century Greek dramatist. In one parable, Aeschylus retold the story of the eagle who was stricken by an arrow. When the eagle looked at the fletching on the arrow's shaft, he said, "With our own feathers, not by other's hands, are we now smitten."

Appendix A

Texas Tech University Administration

As the head football coach, Mike Leach reported to the Athletic Director Gerald Myers, who supervised all of the university's sports programs. Myers reported to President Guy Bailey. Bailey was subordinate to the Texas Tech University System Chancellor Kent Hance and the nine-member Board of Regents. The TTU System includes Texas Tech University, the TTU Health Services Center, and Angelo State University. Compared to the Texas A&M University System with 12 universities and the University of Texas with 9, the Tech System is relatively small.

According to the Tech website, "The government, control, and direction of the university are vested in a nine-member Board of Regents who in turn appoint a Chancellor to carry out the policies of the system as determined by the Regents. The Chancellor appoints a president of each institution in the system. The presidents are chief executive officers of their respective institutions and responsible for the strategic operation of each institution."

Contract

IV.

PERFORMANCE

In the performance of his duties, Coach shall be directly responsible to and under the supervision of the Director of Intercollegiate Athletics. Without limitation of the foregoing, Coach, in the performance of his duties, shall conduct himself at all times in a manner consistent with his position as an instructor of students. The parties agree that, although this Agreement is sports related, the primary purpose of the University and this Agreement is educative. Thus, the educative purposes of the University shall have priority in the various provisions of this Agreement. Coach will follow all applicable University policies and procedures. Coach shall not, either directly or indirectly, breach or countenance the breach by any player or coach subject to his control or supervision of any rules and standard of the Big 12 Conference, the NCAA, youth, collegiate, and master's amateur athletics as well as other associations or agencies to which the University adheres. In this connection, Coach agrees to devote his entire time, labor, effort and attention, in good faith, to conduct and perform the duties commensurate with the position as Head Football Coach, bearing in mind that University recognizes and accepts that Coach has the ability to engage in reasonable Outside Income producing activities as defined in Article III.C.3. Coach shall assure the fair and responsible treatment of student-athletes in relation to their health, welfare, and discipline. Breach of such rules and standards, whether willful or through negligence, may be subject to disciplinary action and penalties ranging from termination, public or private reprimand to monetary fines or adjustments in compensation or adjustments in the term or this contract as determined by the President following consultation and review with the Director of the Intercollegiate Athletics. The provision of the Article IV shall be without prejudice to any right the University may have under Article V of the Agreement.

Unless notice of termination of employment has been given to Coach in accordance with Articles V.A or V.D. below, Coach shall not engage in discussions or negotiate, either directly or indirectly, concerning Coach's prospective employment by any other employer without first providing prior written notice to the Director of Intercollegiate Athletics of such discussion or negotiations. Failure to provide such notice may be considered a material breach of this Agreement.

V.

TERMINATION

A. FOR CAUSE

The University specifically reserves the right to terminate this Agreement for Cause, "Cause" is hereby defined as: Coach's violation of any material provision of this Agreement (with specific reference to Article IV), provided, however, that if such violation is capable of being cured, University shall allow Coach ten (10) business days to cure such violation, provided, however, this if such violation can be reasonably cured, but cannot be cured within ten (10) business days, Coach shall have a reasonable period of time to cure such violation. Notwithstanding Coach's opportunity to cure such violation, Coach shall immediately cease the violating activity upon receipt of notification of such violation from the University. "Cause" shall also include the commission of a major violation or an excessive accumulation of secondary violations of NCAA Legislation ("NCAA Violations") by Coach while at this University or while previously employed at another NCAA member institution; knowingly condoning NCAA Violations by any staff under Coach's direct control and supervision; failure by Coach to take appropriate disciplinary action against such staff member found by Coach to have committed NCAA Violations; failure by Coach to take appropriate disciplinary action against football student-athletes; or indictment of Coach of a criminal act that constitutes a felony, or any misdemeanor involving moral turpitude, under applicable local, state or federal laws.

In the event the University terminates this Agreement for Cause, the University's sole obligation to Coach shall be to pay his Base Salary until the effective date of termination (and any Supplemental Compensation that has been earned pursuant to Article III.C.4 above). In no case shall the University be liable to Coach for the loss of any collateral business opportunities or any other benefits, perquisites, income, Supplemental Compensation, or any form of consequential damages resulting from or associated with Coach's employment.

Texas Tech Statement on Mike Leach Termination
December 30, 2009

After reviewing all the information available, Texas Tech University had decided that the best course of action for the university and its football program is to terminate its relationship with Head Football Coach Mike Leach for cause.

Texas Tech was prepared to participate in the legal proceedings today on Coach Leach's motion for a temporary restraining order. His attorney, however, chose not to participate when he was informed that the termination of Coach Leach was inevitable.

The coach's termination was precipitated by his treatment of a player after the player was diagnosed with a concussion. The player was put at risk for additional injury. After the university was apprised of the treatment, Coach Leach was contacted by the administration of the university in an attempt to resolve the problem. In a defiant act of insubordination, Coach Leach continually refused to cooperate in a meaningful way to help resolve the complaint. He also refused to obey a suspension order and instead sued Texas Tech University. Further, his contemporaneous statements make it clear that the coach's actions against the player were meant to demean, humiliate and punish the player rather than to serve the team's best interest. This action, along with his continuous acts of insubordination, resulted in irreconcilable differences that make it impossible for Coach Leach to remain at Texas Tech.

"It is our number one priority to protect the welfare of our students and the reputation of the Texas Tech University. Parents have entrusted us with their children and we take this responsibility very seriously. We very much appreciate the leadership shown by the university's athletic director, Gerald Myers, and president, Guy Bailey, in dealing with this unfortunate situation. The Board supports their decision," said Larry Anders, Chairman, and Jerry Turner, Vice Chairman of the Texas Tech University Board of Regents.

In the near future, Texas Tech will undertake a search for a new coach. In the meantime, the focus of the athletic department is on preparation for the Valero Alamo Bowl.

Statement by Texas Tech Coach Mike Leach
December 30, 2009

I want everyone to know what a privilege and pleasure it has been to teach and coach more than 400 student-athletes at Texas Tech University over the past 10 years. When I arrived at Texas Tech, the football program was on NCAA probation and the graduation rate was far below the national average. However, in the past 10 years, Tech has been to 10 straight bowl games, has the third best record in the Big 12 Conference, and has the highest graduation rate for football players of any public institution in the county.

Over the past several months, there have been individuals in the Texas Tech administration, Board of Regents and booster groups who have dealt in lies, and continue to do so. These lies have led to my firing this morning. I steadfastly refuse to deal in any lies, and am disappointed that I have not been afforded the opportunity for the truth to be known. Texas Tech's decision to deal in lies and fabricate a story which led to my firing, includes, but is not limited by, the animosity remaining from last year's contract negotiations. I will not tolerate such retaliatory action; additionally, we will pursue all available legal remedies.

These actions taken by Texas Tech have severely damaged my reputation and public image. In addition, Texas Tech has caused harm to not only my family, but to the entire Red Raider nation and the sport of college football.

As you know, I prefer to engage in question and answer sessions; however, in this instance my counsel has advised me to simply make a statement. There will be time to answer questions about this issue in the future, but the serious legal nature of this situation prevents me from going into further detail at this time.

Texas Tech Letter to Leach: December 23, 2009

Dear Coach Leach,

As you know, we have been conducting an inquiry into allegations by a student athlete that your treatment of him, subsequent to his being diagnosed with a mild concussion, may have been injurious to his health and served no medical and/or educational purposes. Texas Tech takes these allegations very seriously. In addition to being unacceptable, if proven, these allegations constitute a breach of your employment contract.

So that we can carry out an inquiry that takes into account the safety of our student athletes and in addition, that is fair to the students, yourself, and the university, we have determined that you must abide by the following guidelines from this day forward.

1. All practices and other team meetings will be monitored by the athletic director or his representative. (Crossed out with the initials GB beside it.)

2. Any player claiming an injury will be examined by a physician and cleared in writing prior to practicing or playing. Decisions regarding whether an injury warrants suspension from practice and/or play will be determined by a physician without pressure from you or your staff.

3. You must recognize that the players you are working with are student athletes and that you have an obligation to treat them with respect and further to conduct yourself in a manner consistent with your position as an instructor of students.

4. You must at all times assure the fair and responsible treatment of student athletes in relation to their health, welfare, and discipline, and if you are not doing so, you must immediately cease any actions not in compliance with this provision of your contract.

5. There will be no retaliation against any student who has suffered an injury.

Again, these allegations are serious, and should they be substantiated will result in disciplinary action ranging from public or private remand, monetary fines or adjustments in compensation, adjustments in the term of this contract, up to termination.

Sincerely,

Guy Bailey

President

Sources/Bibliography

The most important sources used in this work are the sworn depositions of the major participants. Their own words tell the real story. Other court documents are also revealing and are included. Emails also proved helpful. Articles in periodicals contributed as did tapes or transcripts of television and radio shows. Internet search engines, including Google, Bing, and AOL, cite more than a million entries for "Mike Leach Texas Tech." The ones that proved helpful are included. Lastly, personal interviews were most useful. Many individuals, however, agreed to speak only "off the record" and their wishes are honored and their names are not included in this listing. Those who refused to be interviewed are also not listed.

Affidavits

Cantu, Robert T. May 3, 2010
Chisum, Mark "Buzz". April 23, 2010
Hernandez, Grace. April 30, 2010
Phy, Michael. January 1, 2010
Pincock, Stephen. January 1, 2010.
Pincock, Stephen. April 28, 2010 (Supplemental Affidavit)
Sitton, Windy. May 6, 2010
Williams, Jordan. April 23, 2010

Books

James, Craig. *Game Day: A Rollicking Journey to the Heart of College Football.* Hoboken, NJ: Wiley, 2009.

Klosterman, Chuck. *Eating the Dinosaur.* New York: Scribners, 2009.

Leach, Mike. *Swing Your Sword: Leading the Charge in Football and Life.* New York: Diversion Publishing, 2011.

Lewis, Michael. *Moneyball: The Art of Winning an Unfair Game.* New York: W. W. Norton, 2003.

Miller, James Andrew and Tom Shales. *Those Guys Have All the Fun: Inside the World of ESPN.* New York: Little, Brown, 2011.

Myers, Chuck. Foreword by Mike Leach. *The Complete Book of Wide Receivers.* Monterey, CA: Coaches Choice, 2007.

Court Documents

Case No. 2009-550,259: Mike Leach v. Texas Tech University; Kent Hance; Jerry Turner; Larry Anders; Craig James; Guy Bailey; Gerald Myers; and Charlotte Bingham. District Court, 99th Judicial District, Lubbock County, Texas. (This Case No. also includes Leach's motion for a Temporary Restraining Order and Temporary Injunction prior to his termination.)

Case No. 07-10-0247-CV: Mike Leach v. Texas Tech University. Court of Appeals for the Seventh District, Amarillo, Texas.

Case No. 2010554969: Mike Leach v. ESPN and Spaeth Communications, INC. 72nd Judicial District, Lubbock County, Texas.

Case No. 11-0164: Mike Leach v. Texas Tech University. The Supreme Court of Texas.

Depositions
All are from the District Court of Lubbock, Texas, 99th Judicial District

Anders, Larry. March 23, 2010
Bailey, Guy. March 30, 2010
Bingham, Charlotte. March 5, 2010
Hance, Kent. March 11, 2010
James, Adam. March 13, 2010
James, Craig. March 13, 2010
Leach, Mike. March 12, 2010
Myers, Gerald. April 9, 2010
Turner, Jerry E. April 13, 2010

Emails

The emails cited in Chapter 8: "The Turning Point: New Contract Negotiations" are from emails originally secured in an open records request by the *Dallas Morning News.* They can be found in their entirety at the following web site.

http://www.dallasnews.com/sharedcontent/dws/img/12-09/1231newleach.pdf

Other emails are included as exhibits to the various depositions.

Internet Citations

Some internet sites may have expired or been removed by their host. A network search using the article title or subject will generally locate the citation.

"A Look at Mike Leach's Contract."
http://www.kcbd.com/Global/story/asp?S=11742551&clienttype=printable

"A Tribute to Your Joe Morgan Memorial Tournament Winner: Craig James."
http://awfulannouncing.com/2011-articles/july/a-tribute-to-your-joe-morgan-memorial-tournament-winner-craig-james

"Activists Protest Plan to Make West Texas National Nuclear Waste Dumping Ground."
http://lubbockonline.com/texas/2010/12/24/activists-protest-nuclear-waste-plan-west-texas

"Adam James."
http://www.cstv.com/printable/schools/text/sports/m-otbl/mtt/james_adam00.html

"Adam James Stats."
http://sports.espn.go.com.ncf/player/profile?playerId=185042

"Alamo: Most Watched Bowl in ESPN History."
http://espn.go.com/blog/dallas/colleges/print?id=4666022

"Alan B. White."
http://www.plainscapital.com/about-plainscapital/the-chairmans-office

"Another Day, Another Lawsuit Filed by Mike Leach."
http://lubbockonline.com/print/29958

"Another Side to the Leach/Texas Tech Story."
http://www.cbssports.com/print/mcc/blogs/entry/6270202/19274638

"Appellate Court Deals Major Blow to Leach in Case vs. Tech."
http://lubbockonline.com/filed-online/2011-01-21/appellate-court-gives-tech

"ASCO Deal Sparks Conflict."
http://lubbockonline.com/stories/092002/col_0920020029.shtml

"Awful Announcing Final Pits James vs. Buck."
http://www.mediabistro.com/sportsnewser/awful-announcing-final-pits-james-vs-buck

"Blame Bob Knight If Mike Leach Leaves Tx. Tech?"
http://www.sportsbybrooks.com/blame-bob-knight-for-mike-leach-leaving-tech-22300

"Board of Regents."
http://www.texastech.edu/bor/index/php

"Bob Knight."
http://en.wikipedia.org/wiki/Bob_Knight

"Bobby Knight Fouls Out Again."
http://www.thesmokinggun.com/file/bobby-knight-fouls-out-again

"Bowl Team Graduation Rates."
http://marketpower.typepad.com/market_power/2008/12/bowl-team-graduation

"Buddy Holly."
http://en.wikipedia.org/wiki/Buddy_Holly

"Calling the Shots."
http://lubbockonline.com/stories/110202/col_1102020015.shtml

"Captain Leach Gets His Honorary Award."
http://lubbockonline.com/stories/12409/spo_531825923.shml

"Chris Oglesby Interviews Bruce Jaggers."
http://www.virtualubbock.com/intBruce.Jaggers.html

"Clarity Asked for on College Contracts."
http://www.kxan.com/dpp/sports/clarity-asked-for-on-college-contracts

"Coach Leach Goes Deep, Very Deep."
http://www.nytimes.com/2005/12/04/magazine/04coach.html

"Court Rules Against Former Texas Tech Coach Mike Leach."
"http://www.knoxnews.com/news/2011/jan/22/court-rules-against-leach

"Court Rules Against Mike Leach in Lawsuit Against Texas Tech."
http://content.usatoday.com/communities/campusrivalry/post/2011/01/mike-leach-texas-tech

"Craig James."
http://en.wikipedia.org.wiki/Craig_James_(American_football_player)

"Craig James Wants You to Help Texans Save America."
http://awfulannouncing.com/2011-articles/june/craig-james

"Craig James Wins Awful Announcing" Contest."
http:www.mediabistro.com/sportnewser/craig-james-wins-awful-announcing-contest

"David J. Schmidly."
http://en.wikipedia.org.wiki/David_J._Schmidly

"Deadline Passes and Leach Hasn't Signed New Deal With Texas Tech."
http://www.usatoday.com/sports/college/football/big12/2009/02/17-texas-tech

"Death Penalty Killed Football, Saved SMU."
http://www.smudailycampus.com/2.6641/death-penalty-killed-football-saved-smu-1/960307

"Death Penalty (NCAA)."
http://en.wikipedia.org/wiki/Death_Penalty_(NCAA)

"Depositions Continue in Mike Leach Lawsuit."
http://www.kcbd.com/Global/story.asp?S=12134539&clientype=printable

"Doc, Trainer Texas Tech Statements Dated Jan. 1."

http://sportsbybrooks.com/doc-trainer-texas-tech-statements-dated-jan-1-27525

"Donald Trump Introduces Texas Tech Football Team."

http://www.youtube.com/watch?v=szVtpex-8ss

"Emails Provide Deliciously Candid Insights Into Mike Leach's Relationship with TexasTech."

http://deadspin.com/#!5438674/emails-provide-deliciously-candid-insight…

"Eccentric Leach Ready to Lead Red Raiders to Ultimate Treasure."

http://sports.espn.go.com/espn/print?id=3385098&type=Columnist&images

"Emory Blake."

http://www.cstv.com/printfootbl/mtt/blake_emory00

"ESPN Circles the Wagons...Suspends Bruce Feldman."

http://www.conquestchronicles.com/2011/7/14/2276370/espn-circles-the-wagons-suspends-bruce-feldman

"ESPN Denies Suspending College Football Writer for Co-authoring Leach Bio."

http://content.usatoday.com/communities/gameon/post/2011/07/espn-suspends-writer

"ESPN GameDay: Spot on Lubbock, Trump."

http://www.youtube.com/watch?v=xxqfTQwvQRY

"ESPN Ombudsman Says ESPN Coverage of Leach Troubled Him."

http://www.everydayshouldbesaturday.com/2010/01/21/espn-ombudsman-says-espn-coverage-of-leach-troubled-him

"ESPN's Report Tuberville Has Raised $25 million is Wrong."

http://lubbockonline.com/local-news/2010-10-23/espns-report-tuberville-has-raised-25-million-is-wrong

"Ex-BYU Trainer Surrounded by Texas Tech Controversy."

http://www.deseretnews.com/article/print/705356158/Ex-BYU-trainer

"Ex-Tech Players: 'Prima Donna' James Was 'Soft."

http://www.sportsbybrooks.com/ex-tech-players-prima-donna-james-was-soft-27497

"Ex-Tech Regent Sowell Fights Leach Bid for Records."

http://lubbockonline.com/stories/040810/loc_603324322.shtml

"F. Scott Dueser."
http://www.give2tech.com/foundation/directors/scottdueser/

"Federal Investigation of Texas' Radioactive Waste Dump Urged."
http://texasvox.org/2010/08/11/federal-investigation-of-texas

"Feldman, Embattled Writer, Leaves ESPN for CBS."
http://www.nytimes.com/2011/09/02/sports/ncaafootball/feldman

"Firing Leach Saved Tech Buyout Money, But Will Cost It Much More."
http://sportsillustrated.cnn.com/2009/writers/stewart_madel/12/30/

"First Female Mayor."
http://www.lubbockcentennial.com/citysmost/033008.shtml

"Former Players Voice Support for Coach Leach."
http://www.kcbd.com/global/story.asp?s=11745005

"Free Pass."
http://sports.espn.go.com/espn/print?id=3754804&type=Story&images

"Friends, Family Look Back as Myers Retires."
http://www.redraiders.com/2011/05/29/friends-family-look-back-as-myers-retires/

"Game Time: Global Thermonuclear War in Lubbock."
http://blogs.houstonpress.com/hairballs/2009/12/mike_leach_espn_tech.php

"Gamber Named Head Football Athletic Trainer."
http://www.cstv.com/printable/schools/text/sports/m-football/specel/070710aaa.html

"Gerald Myers."
http://en.wikipedia.org/wiki/Gerald_Myers

"Gerald Myers."
http://www.texastech.com/genrel/myers_gerald00.html

"Gerald Myers Announces Retirement From Texas Tech."
http://today.ttu.edu/2010/08/gerald-myers-announces-retirement-from-texas-tech/

"Gerald Myers: Texas Tech Athletic Director vs Coach Mike Leach."
http://www.nowpublic.com/sports/gerald-myers-texas-tech-athletic-director-vs-coach-mike-leach

"Gerald Myers to Leach—No More Money."
http://www.shaggybevo.com/board/showthread.php/23770-gerald-myers-to...

"Gillispie Now Back Where He Belongs."
http://www.chron.com/disp/story/.mpl/sports/solomon/748512.html

"Graham Harrell."
http://wikipedia.org/wiki/Graham_Harrell able/schools/aub/sports/

"Guy Bailey."
http://en.wikipedia.org/wiki//Guy_Bailey

"Hal Mumme."
http://en.wikipedia.org/wiki/Hal_Mumme

"Hance Gives Funds for Chapel."
http://www.dailytoreador.com/news/article_0e2ef9d6-744c-22e0-8d93-
001a4bcf6878.html

"Happiness is Lubbock, Texas in my Rear View Mirror."
http://www.barrypopik.com/index.php/new_york_city/entry/happiness_is

"Harrell, Leach Tour White House."
http://www.redraiders.com/2008/12/13/harrell-leach-tour-white-house

"How Will the 2009-2010 Texas Tech Red Raider Team Fare?"
http://bleacherreport.com/articles/112276-how-will-the-2009-2010-texas-tech

"In Lubbock, a Bizarre Backdrop."
http://thequad.blogs.nytimes.com/2008/11/09/in-lubbock-a-bizarre-backdrop/?

"James Hired Swift Boat Firm Before Going Public."
http://www.sportsbybrooks.com/james-hired-swift-boat-firm-before-going-
public-27593

"James E. Sowell."
http://www.sowellco.com/principals.html

"Jon Whitmore."
http://en.wikipedia.org./wiki/Jon_Whitmore

"Jones AT&T Stadium."
http://en.wikipedia.org/Jones_AT%26T_Stadium

"Judge Sowder Denies Leach's Request for Sanctions."
http://lubbockonline.com/print/11328

"Kent Hance."
http://en.wikipedia.org/wiki/Kent_R._Hance

"Larry K. Anders."
http://www.texastech.edu/bor/bios/anders/php

"Lawsuit Changes Shape; Leach Camp Files Suit Against ESPN."
http://www.dailytoreador.com/news/article_04e8513c2a-11df-aff6-00127992bc8b.html

"Leach Attorney Files Petition to Stop Suspension."
http://www.kcbd.com/Global/story.asp?11743843&clienttype=printable

"Leach Bashes Adam, Craig James on ESPN."
http://www.redraiders.com/2010/01/01/leach-bashes-adam-craig-james-on-espn/

"Leach Denies Cursing Tech Official Before Firing."
http://www.sportsbybrooks.com/leach-denies-cursing-tech-official-before-firing-2605

"Leach Expects Depositions in Texas Tech Suit to Clear His Name.'
http://www.nytimes.com/2010/11/25/sports/ncaafootball/25leach.html

"Leach Hires Law Firm Amid Budget Turmoil."
http://lubbockonline.com/stories/063002/col_0630020024.shtml

"Leach Is Fired Over Treatment of Player."
http://www.nytimes.com/2009/12/31/sports/ncaafootball/31leach.html

"Leach, Myers to Discuss Contract."
http://lubbockonline.com/stories/121802/col_121802013.shtml

"Leach Needs New Strategy, Both on the Field and Off."
http://lubbockonline.com/stories/083102/bur0831020035.shtml

"Leach Only 1 Job Interview in Nine Years."
http://sportsbybrooks.com/emails-leach-only-1-job-interview-in-nine-years-27514

"Leach Returns to West Texas for Book Signing."
http://www.chron.cm/disp/story/mlp/sports/fb/fbc/7660670.html

"Leach Signs Addendum to Contract."
http://lubbockonline.com/stories/121203/col_1212030016.sthml

"Leach Signs Contract."
http://lubbockonline.com/stories/022009/loc_395981525.shtml

"Leach Speaks Out."
http://thequad.blogs.nytimes.com/2009/12/30/leach-speaks-out?

"Leach Sues James-Hired Swift Boat PR Firm, ESPN."
http://www.sportsbybrooks.com/leach-sues-james-hired-swift-boat-pr-firm-espn-29275

"Leach, Tech Formalize Agreement Exempting Individuals From Lawsuit."
http://lubbockonline.com/local-news-/2010-11-24/leach-tech-formalize

"Leach, Tech Reach Five-Year Agreement"
http://sports.espn.go. Com/espn/print?id=3919674&type=story

"Leach, Tech Remain Apart on New Deal."
http://lubbockonline.com/stories/043003/col_043001008.stml

"Leach Timeline."
http://www.redraiders.com/2009/12/31/leach-timeline/

"Leach's Lawyers Fire Back Against Tech."
http://amarillo.com/stories/011310/web_leach.shtml

"Leach's Petition Against ESPN and Spaeth Communications."
http://www.doublenation.com/2010/11/27/1839149/-leachs-petition-against-espn-and-spaeth-communications

"Learning How to Run."
http://partners.nytimes.com/library/politics/camp/072700wh-bush-lubbock-html

"Losing Leach."
http://sportsagentblog.com/2009/02/17/losing-leach/

"Lubbock, Texas."
http://en.wikipedia.org/wiki/Lubbock_Texas

"Lyle Setencich."
http://espn.go.com/blog/big12/tag/_/name/lyle-setencich

"Matt Williams."
http://www.cstv.com/printable/schools/text/sports/m-football/mtt

"Matt Williams."
http://en.wikipedia.org/wiki/Matt_Williams_(American_football

"Nancy Neal."
http://www.texastech.edu/bor/bios/neal.php

"N.C.A.A. Lets Colleges Decide on a Protocol."
http://www.nytimes.com/2009/11/18/sports//ncaafootball/18ncaa

"McNeill Stunned by Leach's Abrupt Firing."
http://espn.go.com/blog/big12/tag/_/name/lyle-setencich

"Merrie Spaeth."
http://www.spaethcom/bios-detail.php?id=1

"Merrie Spaeth Quotes."
http://www.brainyquote.com/quotes/m/merrie_spaeth.html

"Michael Crabtree."
http://wikipedia.org/wiki/Michael_Crabtree

"Mike Leach."
http://en.wikipedia.org/wiki/Mike_Leach

"Mike Leach."
http://www.biographicon.com/view/k243c

"Mike Leach."
http://www.imgspeakers.com/speaker/Bio.aspz?SpeakerID=270

"Mike Leach: Adam James is Lazy, Acts Entitled."
http://www. huffingtonpost.com/2010/01/01/mike-leach-adam-james-is_n_409101.html

"Mike Leach, Coach in Exile, Still Biding His Time in Paradise."
http://cnnsi.printthis.clickability.com/pt/cpt?expire=&title=Mike+Leach+biding+

"Mike Leach Comes to Mark Mangino's Defense."
http://startelegramsports.typepad.com/colleges/2009/11/mike-leach-comes-to

"Mike Leach Creates a Top 9 List."
http://www.footballscoop.com/news/3957-mike-leach-created-a-top-9-list

"Mike Leach Files Lawsuit Against ESPN."
http://sports.espn.go.com/espn/print?id=5847181&type

"Mike Leach Fired."
http://www.huffingtonpost.com/2009/12/30/mike-leach-fired-texas-tech

"Mike Leach Gave Texas Tech Some National Exposure."
http://startelegramsports.typepad.com/colleges/2009/11/mike-leach-gave-texas-tech-some-national-exposure.html#ixzz1Iapi2CFY

"Mike Leach is a Pirate...and a Good Man."
http://ampsportsduo.blogspot.com/2009/12/mike-leach-is-pirateand-good- man.html

"Mike Leach is Thinking...."
http://www.texasmonthly.com/cms/printthis/php?file=features.php&issue=2009-09-01

"Mike Leach: Latest Articles and Videos."
http://www.realclearsports.com/topic/topic.php?topic=Mike_Leach&id=2332&letter

"Mike Leach Lives in Key West, Hoping to Coach Again."
http://washingtonpost.com/sports/college/mike-leach-lives-in-key-west-hoping-to-coach-again

"Mike Leach: Lawsuit Holding Me Back."
http://espn.go.com/blog/dallas/colleges/print?id=4671768

"Mike Leach Named Munger Coach of the Year."
http://www.kcbd.com/story/9533865/mike-leach-named-munger-coach-of-the-year?

"Mike Leach Releases Official Statement to Public."
http://www.sportbybrooks.com/mike-leach-releases-official-statement-to-public-27515

"Mike Leach Responds to His Firing."
http://www.myfoxhouston.com/dpp/sports/091230-mike-leach-firing-reax

"Mike Leach Says Lies Led to Firing."
http://www.tulsaworld.com/site/printerfriendlystory.aspx?articleid=20091231

"Mike Leach Seeks Legislature's Help in Case Against Tech."
http://statesman.com/blogs/content/shared-gen/blogs/austin/enteries/2011/03/11

"Mike Leach Suit Leads to...Another Suit."
http://www.bizjournals.com/dallas/news/2010/12/23/mike-leach-suit-leads

"Mike Leach Takes to Twitter for Rant.'
http://www.lostlettermen.com/6-6-11-mike-leach/

"Mike Leach Taking a Break in Southernmost City."
http://keysnews.com/print/20222

"Mike Leach Testifies in Lawsuit vs Texas Tech."
http://www.theeagle.com/printer/friendly/Mike-Leach-testifies-in-lawsuit-vs-texas-tech

"Mike Leach: The Mad Scientist of Football."
http://www.cbsnews.com/stories/2008/12/31/60minutes/main4694714/shtml

"Mike Leach vs. Texas Tech University: Why It Should Matter to Everyone."
http://bleacherreport.com/articles/325118-mike-leach-texas-tech

"Mike Leach's Attorney Responds to Tech Filings."
http://www.myfoxlubbock.com/mostpopular/story/Mike-Leach-Texas-Tech/oqfoS1PFvU

"Mike Leach's Book Hits Lubbock Book Stores."
http://everythinglubbock.com/fulltext/?nxd_id82287

"Mike Leach's Case Goes Before Texas Legislature."
http://myfoxhouston.com/dpp/sports/local/110311-mike-leach-texas-legislature

"Mike Leach's Offbeat Personality Showed in 2 Years at UK."
http://www.kentucky.com/2008/11/12/588728

"Mike Leach's Wrongful Termination Lawsuit Against Texas Tech Thrown Out by Court."
http://www.sbnation.com/2009/12/28/1222746/mike-leach

"Myers Says Leach Staff Not Reckless."
http://lubbockonline.com/stories/0711020011.shtml

"New Leach Book Lands Bruce Feldman On Suspension."
http://rivals.yahoo.com/ncaa/football/blog/dr_saturday/post/New-Leach-book

"No Flash in the Pan: Texas Tech Looking Like Contenders."
http://espn.go.com/espn/print?id=3691219&type=story

"Obscene Texas Tech Salaries: Kent Hance and Guy Bailey."
http://lubbockcountyregister.blogspot.com/2009/01/obscene-texas-tech-salaries-kent-hance-guy-bailey

"Office of the President Staff."
http://www.ttu.edu/administration/president/staff/php

"Ombudsman Criticizes ESPN's Rules in Review of Reporter's Book."
http://thequad.blogs.nytimes.com/2011/07/19/ombudsman-criticizes-espns-rules in-review-of-reporters-book

"One Fan Knows Softer Sider of Mike Leach."
http://dfw.cbslocal.com/2011/07/26/one-fan-knows-softer-side-of-mike-leach

"193 Mega-Donors Gave Governor Perry $100,000 or More."
http://info.tpj.org/reports/governor2010/Perry100KContributors.html

"Pirate Under Attack: Avast, Ye Swabs!"
http://www.texasmonthly.com/cms/printthis.php?file=webextra.php&issue=2010-01-01

"Police Release Report in Willis Incident."
http://www.myfoxlubbock.com/news/local/story/Willis-Wolfforth-police

"Reality of Andrews County Radioactive Waste Disposal Not What Was Advertised With HB 1567."
http://capitolannex.com/2009/02/22/reality-of-andrews-county-radioactive-waste-disposal-not-what-was-advertised-with-hb-1567

"Record-setting QB Harrell Never Gets Rattled."
http://huskerextra.com/sports/football/article_cd2d58c9-43a6-5f6d-8446-29524ab063de

Report: Ex-Auburn Players Say They Were Paid During Tuberville's Tenure."
http:lubbockonline.com/sports-red-raiders-football/2011-03-31/report-ex-auburn

"Richard Deitsch: Media Circus."
http://cnnsi.printthis.clickabilitly.com/pt/cpt?=&title=Talking+Craig+James%2D=ES

"Rookies Again: At the Craig James Broadcast School."
http://sportsillustrated.cnn.com/vault/article/magazine/MAG1021950/index.htm

"Ruffin McNeill."
http://en.wikipedia.org/wiki/Ruffin_McNeill

"Seth Littrell."
http://www.arizonawildcats.com/sports/m-footbl/mtt/littrell_seth00.html

"Simmons Would Make Billions, Sticking Texas With Nuke Liability."
http://info.tpj.org/Lobby_Watch/simmons.html

"Sitton Email Stokes Fire in Leach Suit."
http://lubbockonline.com/stories/050710/loc_635474108.shtml

"Sitton Says She Was Pressured to Resign."
http://lubbockonline.com/stories/091209/loc_492306870.shtml

"Sources: Tech Owes Former Coach Mike Leach at Least $1.7 Million."
http://www.dallasnews.com/sports/college-sports/texas-tech-red-raiders/20100601

"Sowell Denies Any Year-long Pre-planned Plot to Fire Mike Leach."
http://www.kcbd.com/story/11776556/Sowell-denies

"Spaeth Communications Fires Back at Leach."
http://www.myfoxlubbock.com/mostpopular/story/Spaeth-Communications-ESPN-Leach

"Spaeth Communications, Inc."
http://investing.businessweek.com/research/stocks/private/snapshot.asp?privcapId=22743691

"Spike Dykes."
http://www.texas tech.com/sports/m-footbl/mtt/dykes_spike00

"Spike Dykes."
http://en.wikipedia.org/wiki/Spike_Dykes

"Sports of the Times: At a Salad Bar With Knight, Praise Only the Cherry Tomatoes."
http://www.nytimes.com/2004/02/08/sports/sports-of-the-times-at-a-salad-bar-with-knight

"Statements Contradict Adam James' Version of Events at Texas Tech."
http://www.dallasnews.com/sharedcontent/dws/spt/colleges/texastech/stories/01021dnspont

"Statements from Texas Tech, Leach."
http://www.chron.com/disp/story/mpl/sports/fb/fbc/6793028.html

"Steve Pincock."
http://www.cstv.com/printable/schools/text/sports/mtt/pincock_steve00.html

"Students Have Mixed Reactions to Leach Legal Development."
http://m.lubbockonline.com/sports/2011/01/21/students-have-mixed-reactions

"Swiftboating."
http://en.wikipedia.org/wiki/Swiftboating

"Swift Vets and POWs for Truth."
http://en.wikipedia.org/wiki/Swift_Vets_and_POWs_for-Truth

"Taylor Potts Is Ready To Take Reins in Texas Tech's Red Raider Spread Offense."
http://sports.espn.go.com/ncf/news/story?id=4327472&source=NCFHeadlines

"TCU Extends Gary Patterson Through '18."
http://espn.go.com/espn/print?id=6000665&type

"Team Leach."
http://www.teamleach.org/

"Tech Football Over Budget By Big Sum."
http://lubbockonline.com/stories/062902/col_0629020016.shtml

"Tech, Leach Each Make Concessions on New Contract."
http://lubbockonline.com/stories/041304/upd_777777777.shtml

"Tech Prepares Orphaned Bike Roundup."
http://lubbockonline.com/local-news/2011-05-24/tech-prepares-orphan-bike-roundup

"Tech Regents File Motions for Dismissal."
http://lubbockonline.com/print/10488

"Tech Releases Affidavits That Differ From Statements Produced by Leach Representative."
http://www.dallasnews.com/sports/college-sports/texas-tech-red-raiders/20100102

"Tech's Mike Leach Says OU Has His Vote in Coaches Poll."
http://newsok.com/techs-mike-leach-says-ou-has-his-vote-in-coaches-poll/
article/3324571

"Texas Tech Asst. Coach Now Offers Support to Adam James."
http://usatoday.com/sports/college/football/big12/2009-12-31-lincoln-riley

"Texas Tech Board of Regents Approve Budget; 600 Jobs Lost."
http://www.kcbd.com/story/15219739/texas-tech-board-of-regents-approve-
smallest-budget

"Texas Tech Coach Credits Old Dog for His New Tricks."
http://signonsandiego.printthis.clickability.com/pt/cpt?expire=&title=Texas+Tech+c
oach+credits

"Texas Tech Coach Mike Leach: Quotes."
http://boards.kusports.com/showflat.php?Cat=0&number=1189785&Main=1189068

"Texas Tech Fans Embrace Hocutt, Gillispie."
http://www.star-telegram.com/2011/05/29/v-print/3111536/texas-tech-fans-
embrace-hocutt-gillispie

"Texas Tech: Leach Firing Causes Academic Cuts."
http://sportsbybrooks.com/tech-faces-academic-cuts-because-of-leach-firing-27574

"Texas Tech, Mike Leach Finally Agree to Contract Extension."
http://collegesportsblog.dallasnews.com/archives/2009/02/texas-tech

"Texas Tech Quarterbacks Under Mike Leach."
http://www.cbssports.com/collegefootball/story/11070145

"Texas Tech Red Raiders Fire Mike Leach."
http://sports.espn.go.com/ncf/bowls09/news/story?id=4781981

"Texas Tech Red Raiders Football."
http://en.wikipedia.org/wiki/Texas_Tech_Red_Raiders_fooball

"Texas Tech Regent Jerry Turner Responds to Leach Lawsuit."
http://myfoxlubbock.com/news/local/story/Jerry-Turner

"Texas Tech Regent Larry Anders Files Answer to Leach Lawsuit."
http://www.myfoxlubbock.com/news/local/story/Larry-Anders

"Texas Tech Suspends Leach."
http://thequad.blogs.nytimes.com/2009/12/28/texas-tech-suspends-leach/?

"Texas Tech: The Mike Leach Era."
http://hubpages.com/hub/texastechmikeleachera

"Texas Tech to Build Hance Chapel on Campus."
http://today.ttu.edu/2011/05/texas-tech-to-build-hance-chapel-on-campus/

"Texas Tech Trainer Steve Pincock Says Adam James is Liar."
http://www.associatedcontent.com/shared/print/.shtml?content

"Texas Tech 2009 Football Predictions."
http://www.betfirms.com/texas-tech-football-predictions-2009/

"Texas Tech University."
http://en.wikipedia.org/wiki/Texas_Tech

"Texas Tech vs. Texas Game Moved to September 19."
http://today.ttu.edu/2009/02/texas-tech-vs-texas-game-moved-to-september/

"Texas Tech's Secret? There are None."
http://thequad.blogs.nytimes.com/2008/11/22/texas-techs-secret-there-are-none

"The Mike Leach Firing: Someone is Lying."
http://www.huffingtonpost.com/ed-berliner/-the-mike-leach-firing-som_b_407702l.
html?

"The Mike Leach, Texas Tech Soap Opera."
http://soonerguys.com/blog/?p=54

"The Saga of Mike Leach and Texas Tech: Contract Negotiations."
http://www.doubletnation.com/2009/2/7/752291/the-saga-of-mike-leach-and

"The Unhireable Mike Leach."
http://dev.chuckoliver.net/2011/06/the-unhireable-mike-leach/

"The West Texas Waste Wars."
http://www.texasradiation.org/andrews/wastewar.html

**"Timeline of Texas Tech Coach Mike Leach's Contract Extension
Negotiations."**
http://collegesportsblog.dallasnews.com/archives/2009/02/timeline-of

"Tuberville Miserable at Tech."
http://www.doubletnation.com/2011/3/23/2067896/sportsbybrooks

"Tuberville Raise Rankles Tech Faculty."
http://lubbockonline.com/local-news/2011-02-21/tuberville-raise-rankles-tech-faculty

"20 Texas Tech Officials Gone in 29 Months."
http://newsradio1420.com/newsradio/newsmaker.asp?storyID=14152

"2008 Texas Tech Red Raiders Football Team."
http://en.wikipedia.org/wiki/2008_Texas_Tech_Red_Raiders_football_team

"2008 Texas vs. Texas Tech Football Game."
http://en.wikipedia.org/wiki/2008_Texas_vs._Texas_Tech_football_game

"2009 Cotton Bowl Classic."
http://en.wikipedia.org/wiki/2009_Cotton_Bowl_Classic

"2009 Big 12 Conference Football Season."
http://en.wikipedia.org/wiki/2009_Big_12_Conference_football_season

"2009 Texas Tech Red Raider Football Team."
http://en.wikipedia.org/wiki/2009_Texas_Tech_Red_Raider_football_team

"Updated: Mike Leach Suing ESPN."
http://lubbockonline.com/filed-online/2010-11-24/mike-leach-suing-espn

"University Release Affidavits."
http://espn.go.com/espn/print?id=4790586&tpye=headlinenews&imagesprint

"Video: Craig James in 'Spiritual War' With Leach."
http://www.sportsbybrooks.com/craig-james-in-spirtual-war-with-mike-leach-28322

"Watch Your Assets: Exposing the Misuse and Abuse of the Public Commons."
http://info.tpj.org/watchyourassets/housing/index/html

"Well Appointed Public Officials."
http://info.tpj.org/docs/2000/10/reports/appointments/appendix.html

"What Mike Leach Learned (Opps) in Law School."
http://sport-law.blogspot.com/2010/01/what-mike-leach-learned-opps-in-law

"What Tommy Tuberville Won't Like About Texas Tech and It May Be Mutual."
http://bleacherreport.com/articles/323293-what-tommy-tubeville-won't-like-about-texas-tech-and-it-may-be-mutual

"Why I Love Mike Leach, Graham Harrell, and Texas Tech."
http://www.pitchershiteighth.com/2008/12/01/why-i-love-mike-leach-graham-harrell-and-texas-tech

"Why is Mike Leach Really Suing ESPN?"
http://www.sportsbybrooks.com/realtalk-why-is-mike-leach-really-suing-espn-29276

"Why Won't Anyone Hire Mike Leach?"
http://sportsillustrated.cnn.com/2011/writers/stewart_mandel/01/19/mike.leach/index.html

"Youth Football the Texas Tech Mike Leach Way."
http://football191286.wordpress.com/2011/04/16/youth-football-the-texas-tech-mike-leach-way

Interviews
(Personal, telephone, and email)

Amendola, Danny. April 4, 2011
Blaney, Betsy. July 29, 2011
Christy, Pete. April 11, 2011
Clark, James. April 6, 2011
Cook, Chris. May 20, 2011; September 2, 2011; September 10, 2011
Crabtree, Michael. June 13, 2011
Dean, Bill. April 6, 2011
Feldman, Bruce. September 6, 2011
Ford, Butch. June 23, 2011
Ghaddar, J. R. June 27, 2011
Hodges, Charlie. May 17, 2011
Klotzman, Jeff. June 11, 2011
Krulewitz, Josh. July 29, 2011

Lanning, Reveilee. April 15, 2011
McLaughlin, Scott. August 2, 2011
Parrish, Curtis. May 27, 2011
Ross, Patty. September 13, 2011
Ross, Phill. June 26, 2011
Walker, Dave. June 23, 2011
Watson, Skip. April 14, 2011
Wheelan, Dr. Belle S. September 14, 2011

Polls

"Findings From West Texas Voter Poll." Washington, D. C.: Lincoln Park Strategies, March 4, 2011.

"Texas Tech University Survey Results." Irving, TX: NASICA Consulting Services, September 21, 2011.

Public Documents Surrounding the Mike Leach Litigation

Many of the public documents concerning the 2008-09 contract negotiations and the 2009-present termination are posted on the website of the *Lubbock Avalanche-Journal* and can be found at http://lubbock online.com/print/34267.

Southern Association of Colleges and Schools (SACS)

"The Principles of Accreditation: Foundations for Quality Enhancement." 4th edition. 2009.

State of Texas Documents

"Texas Education Code." Chapters 109 and 110. November 2009.

Texas Tech University Documents

"Employment Contract Between Texas Tech University and Mike Leach." February 19, 2009.

"Texas Tech University Regents' Rules and Policy Statements." December 12, 2008.
"Texas Tech University Policies and Procedures OP 70.31." September 22, 2004

Videos

The so called "electric closet" video released by Spaeth Communications can be viewed at:
http://www.youtube.com/watch?v=dZqvajnhADU

A video tour of the equipment garage and media room is at;
http://rbabe.com/musings/video-of-coach-mike-leachs-torture-shed/336

SMU and the "Death Penalty" are covered in:
http//at::://30for30.espn.com/film/pony-excess.html

The Leach locker room video following the narrow Baylor victory in November 2009 cam be found by searching YouTube for "Mike Leach After the Baylor Game" or at:
http://www.doublenation.com/2010/3/11/1368965/mike-leach-post-game-thoughts

About the Author

Michael Lee Lanning is the author of eighteen non-fiction books. Three of his military history books, the genre for which he is best known, have been translated into a total of eleven languages in thirteen countries. He has sold more than a million copies of his works in print, audio, and e-book formats. Various editions have been included in the Military Book Club. His books have been reviewed in publications as diverse as the *New York Times, The Sunday Times of London, Infantry Magazine,* and *Soldier of Fortune.* The *New York Times Book Review* called Lanning's *Vietnam 1969-1970: A Company's Commander's Journal,* "…one of the most honest and horrifying accounts of a combat soldier's life to come out of the Vietnam War."

Lanning was born in Sweetwater, Texas, and raised on a West Texas stock farm. He earned a bachelor's degree from Texas A&M University and a master's from East Texas State University. He is a retired U.S. Army lieutenant colonel who served in the Vietnam War as an infantry platoon leader, reconnaissance platoon leader, and rifle company commander.

He currently resides on the Bolivar Peninsula on the Texas Gulf Coast.

Made in the USA
Lexington, KY
01 December 2012